CW01045238

# THE CHRONICLE

OF

# ADAM OF USK

# THE CHRONICLE

OF

# ADAM OF USK

## A.D. 1377–1421

EDITED
WITH A TRANSLATION AND NOTES

BY

SIR EDWARD MAUNDE THOMPSON, K.C.B.

Second edition, Henry Frowde, 1904.

Facsimile reprint of the English translation,
with an abridged introduction.
Llanerch Enterprises, 1990.

There are three several subjects of interest which, before all others, form the most prominent features in Adam's work: the fall and deposition of Richard; the occurrences at Rome during the period of the writer's residence there; and the rebellion of Owen Glendower and contemporary affairs in Wales.

The detailed account of Richard's last parliament in 1397, with which the continuous historical narrative practically leads off, is borrowed from the chronicle of the Monk of Evesham; but this appropriation, it is fair to suggest, need not be regarded so much as a theft as a testimony to the accuracy of that history, Adam himself having been present during the proceedings. It is also Adam's personal share in the subsequent events which culminated in Richard's deposition that renders his account of things at this time so valuable as well as interesting.

His compulsory sojourn at Rome happened at an important period of papal history—the period of the death of Boniface the ninth, and of the succession of Innocent the seventh and his quarrel with the Romans and his flight from the city and subsequent return. These events afford our chronicler an opportunity for describing various public ceremonies, which naturally had an attraction for him as a stranger, and of which he gives some curious details.

But, as a Welshman, Adam takes special notice of events in his native country, and his account of the progress of Glendower's rebellion contains many details of value. Although he speaks of the national hero and his following with some contempt, at the same time he evinces a natural sympathy with the sufferings of his countrymen at the hands of the invading English; and, as already observed, the fact of his taking refuge with Glendower, while in disgrace with Henry, after his return from Rome, suggests an earlier understanding between them. Perhaps it was to some connection of this nature that Adam owed his knowledge of Owen's letters of appeal to the king of Scotland and the Irish chieftains, which he incorporates in his chronicle.

Other documents of interest of which Adam gives the text are: sir Thomas Dymock's petition for the championship at the coronation of Henry the fourth; the case submitted for Adam of Usk's opinion on the question of the restoration of queen Isabella's dower; and the letter of remonstrance addressed to Henry the fourth by his confessor Philip Repyngdon, the abbot of Leicester.

# THE CHRONICLE

OF

# ADAM OF USK

Our gracious king Edward departing this life on the eve A.D. 1377.
of the Nativity of Saint John Baptist[1], in the fifty-second
year of his reign, Richard, son of Edward, prince of Wales,
the eldest son of king Edward—a boy of eleven years, and
fair among men as another Absalom—came to the throne,
and was crowned at Westminster on Saint Kenelm's day[2].

During this king Richard's reign great things were looked
for. But he being of tender years, others, who had the care
of him and his kingdom, did not cease to inflict on the
land acts of wantonness, extortions, and unbearable wrongs.
Whence sprang that unnatural deed, when the commons of A.D. 1381.
the land, and specially those of Kent and Essex, under their
wretched leader Jack Straw[3], declaring that they could no
longer bear such wrongs, and above all wrongs of taxes and
subsidies, rose in overwhelming numbers against the lords
and the king's officers, and, marching to London on the eve
of Corpus Christi (12th June), in the year of Our Lord

---

[1] This date is not correct. Edward III. died on the Sunday next
before the feast of the Nativity of St. John the Baptist, the 21st of
June, 1377, not on the eve of the feast, the 23rd of the month; and
in the fifty-first, not the fifty-second, year of his reign.

[2] More correctly, the eve of St. Kenelm, the 16th July.

[3] Wat Tyler is quite lost sight of. Knighton (Rolls series, ij. 137),
in like manner, confuses the two men: " ductor eorum proprio nomine
Watte Tyler, sed jam nomine mutato vocatus est Jakke Strawe."

1381, struck off the heads of Simon Sudbury, archbishop of Canterbury, then the king's chancellor, sir Robert Hales, the treasurer, and many others, hard by the Tower of London. And on the places where these lords were beheaded there are set up to this day two marble crosses, a lasting memorial of so monstrous a deed.

In this rising of the commons were many great men of the land in many places beheaded. The Savoy, the palace of the duke of Lancaster and the fairest in the kingdom, standing near London on the bank of Thames, was, from the commons' hatred of the duke, utterly destroyed by them with fire; and the duke himself, for fear of them, fled into Scotland[1]. To appease them and to quiet their fury, the king granted that the state of villeinage, as well in their persons as in their labour, should be henceforth done away, freedom fully given, and all prisoners set at large. And this he commanded and made to be openly proclaimed throughout the counties of the kingdom. And then what a throe of grief passed through the desolated land! For they boasted that they would slay all those of higher birth, would raise up king and lords from among themselves, would stablish new laws, and, in a word, would make new, or rather disfigure, the face and estate of the whole island. Then every man struck off the head of his enemy, and despoiled his richer neighbour. But, by the mercy of God, when their leader, being in Smithfield near London, doffed not his hood before the king nor in anything did reverence to the king's majesty, his head was deftly struck off, in the very midst of his flock of kites, by sir William Walworth,

---

[1] John of Gaunt was at this time in the north, negotiating a truce with Scotland. Knighton (ij. 143-7) tells us that so unpopular was his name that his duchess was refused admission into his own castle at Pontefract, and that he himself was denied hospitality by the earl of Northumberland; and that it was reported that a large force of the insurgents was sent north in pursuit of him. He retired to Edinburgh on a safe-conduct from the Scots, by whom he was well entertained.

knight and citizen of London; and straightway, being
raised on the point of a sword, it was shown before them.
Then the commons in sore dread sought flight by stealth,
and there and then casting away their rebellious weapons,
as though unguilty of such riot and wickedness, like foxes
into their holes, they pitifully crept home. But the king and
the lords pursued them, and some they made to be dragged
behind horses, some they slew with the sword, some they
hanged on the gallows, some they quartered; and they
destroyed thousands [1].

In this same year there came into England one Pileus [2],
cardinal priest of Saint Praxedes, to treat, on behalf of
the emperor of Germany and king of Bohemia, with the
council of England of and about a marriage between our
king and the lady Ann, sister of the same emperor [3]; who
afterwards became thereby our most gracious queen, howbeit
she died without issue. At his coming, this cardinal,
falsely feigning himself legate *a latere* and as having the
power of the pope, then did exercise the papal offices.
And among other things he made me notary, though to no

---

[1] The severity of the punishments inflicted after the suppression of
the outbreak is fully set forth in the pages of Walsingham's History.
Richard, however, interfered to prevent indiscriminate slaughter of
the insurgents when first beaten in the field.—Wals. *Hist. Angl.* (Rolls
series), i. 466.

[2] Pileo di Prata, bishop of Padua, and, in 1370, archbishop of
Ravenna. He was one of the papal legates employed, at Bruges, in
negotiating a peace between England and France, in 1375. At the
papal schism, in 1378, he threw in his lot with Urban VI., by whom
he was made cardinal, and was sent nuncio to Germany. In 1386, he
seceded to Clement VII., who employed him in an unsuccessful attempt
to break the power of Urban in Florence. But three years after, on
the death of Urban, he deserted Clement for Boniface IX., who made
him cardinal bishop of Tusculum. By these agile changes he got the
nickname of "Cardinalis trium Pileorum," the Cardinal of Three
Hats. He was further appointed legate at Viterbo; but he exas-
perated the people to such a degree that they drove him out. He
died in 1401.—Ciaconius, *Vitæ Pont. Rom.* ij. 637.

[3] Wenceslaus, or Wenzel, emperor of Germany, 1378.

A.D. 1381. purpose, in the house of the friars preachers of London, where he was then dwelling. Thus did he gather to himself countless money, and, the treaty of marriage being settled, he departed from England with his gains, to his own condemnation; idly trusting that the pope would A.D. 1382. approve these his acts. And, after his departure, the said lady Ann was bought for a great price by our lord the king, for she was much sought in marriage by the king of France[1]; and she was then sent over into England to be crowned queen.

According to the saying of Solomon: "Woe to thee, O land, when thy king is a child,"[2] in the time of the youth of the same Richard many misfortunes, both caused thereby and happening therefrom, ceased not to harass the kingdom of England, as has been before said and as will hereinafter more fully appear, even to the great disorder of the state and to the last undoing of king Richard himself and of those who too fondly clung to him. Amongst all other misfortunes, nay, amongst the most wicked of all wicked things, even errors and heresies in the catholic faith, England, and above all London and Bristol[3], stood corrupted, being infected by the seeds which one master John Wycliffe

[1] This is not stated by the other chroniclers. The idea was no doubt suggested by the intention of the king of France, Charles V., to waylay and capture her on the sea, out of hostility to England. He desisted on the remonstrance of Ann's uncle, the duke of Brabant. Ann landed in England on the 18th December, 1381, and was married on the 14th January, 1382. Knighton (ij. 150) says:— "dedit imperatori, ut dicebatur, pro maritagio decem mille libras, præter alias expensas in quærendo eam et adducendo eam sumptibus suis propriis."

[2] Eccles. x. 16.

[3] Adam of Usk, as a native of Monmouthshire, would naturally take an interest in what went on in the neighbouring city of Bristol. John Purvey, Wycliffe's follower and part-translator of the Bible, preached there; and it is not improbable that Wycliffe himself also did so, as, in 1375, he was presented by Edward III. to the prebend of Aust, in the collegiate church of Westbury-on-Trym.—Seyer, *Memoirs of Bristol*, ij. 164.

sowed, polluting as it were the faith with the tares of his A.D. 1382.
baleful teaching. And the followers of this master John,
like Mahomet, by preaching things pleasing to the powerful
and the rich, namely, that the withholding of tithes and
even of offerings and the reaving of temporal goods from
the clergy were praiseworthy, and, to the young, that
self-indulgence was a virtue, most wickedly did sow the
seed of murder, snares, strife, variance, and discords, which
last unto this day, and which, I fear, will last even to the
undoing of the kingdom. Whence, in many parts of the
land, and above all in London and in Bristol, they, like
the Jews at Mount Horeb on account of the molten calf
(Exodus xxxij.), turning against each other, righteously
had to grieve for three-and-twenty thousand of their fellows
who suffered a miserable fate[1]. The people of England,
wrangling about the old faith and the new, are every day,
as it were, on the very point of bringing down upon their
own heads rebellion and ruin. And I fear that in the end
it will happen as once it did, when many citizens of London
true to the faith rose against the duke of Lancaster to slay
him, because he favoured the said master John, so that,
hurrying from his table into a boat hastily provided, he
fled across Thames and hardly escaped with his life[2]. Such
errors and heresies grew in the city of London to so great
a height (seeing that from such cause spring strife and
variance), that, when such as were accused thereof came
to answer before their ordinaries, the people were wont

---

[1] The round number of 23,000 may be intended to represent the
total of sufferers down to the time when the chronicle was finished,
that is, towards the close of the reign of Henry V.

[2] In February, 1377, when Wycliffe appeared in St. Paul's to answer
the charges brought against him. A quarrel arising between the
duke of Lancaster, who was present as a supporter of Wycliffe, and
William Courtenay, bishop of London, the duke made use of violent
language, which roused the anger of the Londoners, who attacked
the Savoy and would have done the duke mischief, had he not
escaped by boat on the Thames.—Walsingham, *Hist.* i. 325 ; *Archæo-
log.* xxij. 256 ; *Chronicon Angliæ*, 1328–1388 (Rolls series), 119, 397.

A.D. 1382.  to run together in thousands, some accusing, others defending, them, with clamour and strife, as if they were just rushing at each other's throats[1].  So great, too, grew their malice, that, at the time of the second parliament of king Henry the fifth, hereinafter written, these Lollards, flocking to London from all parts of the land, thought to have utterly destroyed the clergy there at that time assembled[2]. But my lord of Canterbury, forewarned of their evil design, found fitting remedies, as will hereinafter be told.

A.D. 1386.  Owing to the many ill-starred crises of king Richard's reign, which were caused by his youth, a solemn parliament was holden at Westminster, wherein twelve of the chief men of the land were advanced, by full provision of parliament, to the government of the king and the kingdom, in order to bridle the wantonness and extravagance of his servants and flatterers, and, in short, to reform the business of the realm; but alas! only to lead to the weary deeds which are hereinafter written[3].

[1] Compare the passage in Walsingham : "Insuper nec illud esse silendum æstimo, cum episcopi prædicti cum isto schismatico in capella archiepiscopi apud Lambhith convenissent, non dico cives tantum Londonienses, sed viles ipsius civitatis, se impudenter ingerere præsumpserunt in eandem capellam, et verba facere pro eodem, et istud negotium impedire."—*Hist. Angl.* i. 356, ij. 65.

[2] The MS. reads "Henrici quarti," but this is a clerical blunder, The gathering in St. Giles's-fields, under sir John Oldcastle, is referred to.  But Adam is not accurate : the actual date of the rising was in January, while Henry the fifth's second parliament, which was held at Leicester, did not meet till April, 1414.  See below, p. 300.

[3] The actual number of the commissioners appointed by the Wonderful Parliament of 1386 was eleven, or fourteen if the three principal officers of state be included.  The eleven were : the archbishops of Canterbury and York, the dukes of York and Gloucester, the bishops of Winchester and Exeter, the abbot of Waltham, the earl of Arundel, John de Cobham, Richard le Scrope, and John Devereux.  Thomas Arundel, bishop of Ely, had replaced Michael de la Pole, earl of Suffolk, as chancellor ; John Gilbert, bishop of Hereford, was treasurer ; and John de Waltham, keeper of the privy seal.  It will be remembered that John of Gaunt was at this time in Spain, as a reason for his name not appearing on the commission.

The king, bearing it ill that by this appointment the due A.D. 1387. freedom of his majesty should be bridled by his own lieges, and urged by his servants who were angered that their evil gains were thereby prevented, ceased not to thwart those who were thus set in authority, till the end came in the destruction of the king himself, his abettors, and many of these same rulers. And from thence alas! what griefs and weary deeds followed, and specially concerning the death of those nobles, the duke of Gloucester and the earl of Arundel, it will appear more fully hereafter. To proceed: those who thus urged on the king, in order to the sudden suppression of the twelve rulers, planned that a general council should be holden in the Tower of London, wherein they thought suddenly and at one blow, by means of an ambush of armed men, to destroy the twelve when summoned to, the council. But the Almighty disposed the twelve, being forewarned of that wicked design, to come in such strength that the king and his abettors, disordered by their warlike preparation, feared that the kingdom would rise in their favour. Wherefore a peace was made, though a hollow one. Hearing this, our lady the princess, the mother of the king, with heavy grief in her heart, and not sparing to toil on even by night, hastened from Wallingford to London, to allay the discord. And on her knees she prayed the king, her son, as he looked for her blessing, in no wise to bend to the wishes of flatterers, and specially of those who were now urging him on; otherwise he would bring down her curse upon him. But the king with reverence raised her up and promised that he would willingly be guided by the counsel of the twelve. To whom his mother replied: "At thy coronation, my son, I rejoiced that it had fallen to my lot to be the mother of an anointed king; but now I grieve, for I foresee the fall which threatens thee, the work of accursed flatterers." Then the king passed with his mother to Westminster Hall, and there, seated on his throne of state, by her mediation,

A.D. 1387. made his peace with the twelve guardians; yet did he it falsely and with deceit[1].

Soon afterwards, the earl of Oxford[2] went with royal letters into the county of Chester, and led back with him a great armed power of the men of those parts, for the destruction of the twelve. But the duke of Gloucester and

[1] Adam has here mixed up several events in confusion. He tells us further on that we must not read this earlier part of his chronicle as consecutive history; and the hint is wanted nowhere more than in this his account of Richard's attempt to cast off the thraldom in which the Wonderful Parliament had placed him. The stories of plots laid by Richard for the destruction of his enemies are so many, and told in so many different ways in the chronicles, that some confusion in the mind of the writer may be pardoned. Knighton (ij. 216) first reports the rumour that the king, who had retired to Eltham on the meeting of the parliament, in 1386, designed to assassinate a deputation of forty of the members whom he had summoned to appear before him. Walsingham (ij. 150) records a plot to invite the duke of Gloucester and the parliamentary opponents of the earl of Suffolk to a banquet in the city, and there slay them. The Monk of Evesham (75) repeats this story, adding, "Michael statuit (ne dicam, hoc esse regis commentum)." The commons themselves, in their petition against the duke of Ireland's party, refer to some such design, saying that the traitors "firent que nostre seigneur le Roi commanda a Meire de Loundre de faire sudeinement lever un graunt poare de gentz de Loundre, d'occire et mettre au mort touz les ditz seigneurs et communs horpris ceux qui furrunt de lour coveine" (Rot. Parl. iij. 231, art. 15). Again, in 1387, after the council of Nottingham, when the revolted lords were invited by Richard to a conference at Westminster, they advanced with extreme caution on the report of an ambush in the Mews (Wals. ij. 165; Mon. Evesh. 91; Knighton, ij. 248). Unfortunately for the story of the intervention of the princess of Wales, that lady had already died in 1385. However, the fact remains that, not long before her death, she did undertake a fatiguing journey to reconcile Richard with his uncle, the duke of Lancaster; though the words which are placed in her mouth by our chronicler are not recorded elsewhere (Wals. ij. 126; Mon. Evesh. 60).

[2] Robert de Vere, earl of Oxford, created successively marquess of Dublin and duke of Ireland. He was killed while hunting at Louvain, in 1392. Richard had his body brought to England, and opened the coffin in order to gaze upon the dead features of his favourite. The earl was buried with great honours at Colne priory in Essex.

the earls of Derby, Arundel, Nottingham, and Warwick, A.D. 1387. were forewarned thereof, and arrayed in a glorious host, before the men of Chester could reach the king, they routed the earl's army on the eve of Saint Thomas the Apostle (20th December), at Radcot-bridge in Oxfordshire. And the earl himself they drove in flight beyond hope of return ; for he died beyond seas.   Then, too, fled before the face of the lords Alexander Nevill, archbishop of York, and the lord Michael de la Pole, earl of Suffolk, the king's chief councillors ; and they came not back, but died in exile [1].

At that time, I, the writer of this chronicle, was at Oxford, an " extraordinary " in canon law, and I saw the host of the five lords march through the city on their way to London from the battle-field ; whereof the earls of Warwick and Derby led the van, the duke of Gloucester the main body, and the earls of Arundel and Nottingham the rear.

The mayor of London, hearing of their coming, sent forth to them the keys of the city ; and thereafter those same five lords did, on the feast of Saint John the Evangelist (27th December), blockade the Tower [2] of London till it yielded ; then straightway they placed the king, who lay A.D. 1388. therein, under new governance, and delivered his fawning councillors into divers prisons until the next following parliament [2].   On the morrow of the Purification of Our

---

[1] Alexander Nevill, archbishop of York, on his attainder, was translated by pope Urban to the see of St. Andrew's. This dignity was, however, worth no more than a bishopric *in partibus*, as Scotland followed Clement VII. The archbishop showed his wisdom by retiring to a small cure at Louvain, where he died in 1392.

Suffolk went first to Holland, but was afterwards invited to Paris, where he died in 1389.  Walsingham (ij. 187) cannot find words bad enough for this able minister of Richard II.  A good sketch of his administration, viewed in a favourable light, will be found in the work of M. Wallon, *Richard II.* (Paris, 1864).

[2] The confederate lords entered London on the 26th December, and immediately invested the Tower.  Richard submitted, and summoned parliament to meet on the 3rd February.

A.D. 1388. Lady (3rd February), they declared exiles those who had fled, and they banished into Ireland all the king's justices, for that they had knowledge of the imagining of the death of the lords, as above written, and also the king's confessor, the bishop of Chichester[1]. Others who had wrongfully fostered the king's unruliness, if not the causers thereof, namely, sir Simon Burley, chamberlain, sir Robert Tresilian, chief justice, Nicholas Brembre, mayor of London, sir John Berners and sir John Salisbury, knights, and Thomas Usk and John Blake, esquires, and very many others were beheaded[2].

A.D. 1383. In this king's reign, on account of the papal schism, the bishop of Norwich[3] crossed over into Flanders with a

[1] The judges who had taken a part in the council of Nottingham were—sir Robert de Belknap, chief justice of the Common Pleas; sir Robert de Fulthorp, sir John Holt, and sir William Burgh, puisne judges of the same; sir John Cary, junior baron of the Exchequer; and with them, John Lokton, serjeant-at-law. Belknap and Holt were banished to Drogheda, Fulthorp and Burgh to Dublin, Cary and Lokton to Waterford. Thomas Rushook, bishop of Chichester and the king's confessor, was sent to Cork.—Rymer, *Fœdera*, 8th and 13th July, 1388.

[2] The execution of sir Simon Burley, the retainer of the Black Prince and Richard's tutor, which was carried out in spite of all the king's efforts to save him, made an impression on Richard's mind which goes far to account for the fierceness with which he attacked his enemies in the parliament of 1397. Berners and Salisbury (as well as sir John Beauchamp, who was also executed) were of the royal household. Thomas Usk had been appointed under-sheriff of Middlesex, with the view of influencing the elections to parliament; and John Blake had been commissioned to draw the bill of indictment which Richard, had he not been forestalled, would have brought forward against the confederate lords, in 1387, after the council of Nottingham. Usk has recently risen into a more interesting position than that which he holds in history, having been identified as the author of "The Testament of Love," a work which has been wrongly attributed to Chaucer. (*Dict. Nat. Biogr.* lviij. 60; Skeat, *Chaucerian and other Pieces*, 1897.)

[3] Henry Spencer or Despencer, the warlike bishop of Norwich, had fought in his youth for pope Adrian against Bernabo Visconti of Milan, and received for his reward the see of Norwich in 1370. But "vulpis pilum mutat, non animum," and the bishop did not lose his

crusade, and there he destroyed in warfare some nine A.D. 1383. thousand men of that land who sided with the French heretics; but he was forced to withdraw thence and to return to his own country by the power of the king of France and his army, many of the English then dying of the flux.

The duke of Lancaster also, claiming the kingdom of A.D. 1386 -1388. Spain in right of his wife, sailed to that country two years after, with another crusade; and there he lost by the same sickness many of the nobles of the realm of England, and, I may say, the flower of its youthful chivalry. Yet he made peace with the king of Spain, receiving a duchy for the term of his life, and a large sum of gold for his outlay, and giving his daughter in marriage to the king's eldest son; and so he returned to England [1].

In these days there happened at Oxford a grave mis- A.D. 1388 fortune. For, during two whole years was there great strife between the men of the south and the men of Wales on the one side and the northerners on the other. Whence arose broils, quarrels, and ofttimes loss of life. In the first year the northerners were driven clean away from the university. And they laid their expulsion chiefly to my charge. But in the second year, in an evil hour, coming back to Oxford, they gathered by night, and denying us passage from our quarters by force of arms, for two days they strove sorely against us, breaking and plundering some of the halls of our side, and slaying certain of our men. Howbeit, on the third day our party, bravely

taste for fighting. He was distinguished at the time of Wat Tyler's rebellion for the vigour with which he repressed the uprising in his diocese: defeating, shriving, and executing the rebels with great zeal. His crusade in Flanders got him into trouble, for he had to pay the penalty of failure by the loss of his temporalities, which were, however, afterwards restored.—Godwin, *De Præsul. Angl.*

[1] There is no mention of the duchy in the other chronicles. By the terms of the treaty, Catherine of Lancaster married Henry, prince of the Asturias, in 1393. The duke received the sum of 200,000 crowns and a pension for the lives of himself and his duchess.

A.D. 1388,
1389.

strengthened by the help of Merton Hall, forced our
adversaries shamefully to fly from the public streets, which
for the two days they had held as a camp, and to take
refuge in their own quarters.  In short, we could not be
quieted before many of our number had been indicted for
felonious riot; and amongst them I, who am now writing,
was indicted, as the chief leader and abettor of the Welsh,
and perhaps not unrighteously.  And so indicted we were
hardly acquitted, being tried by jury before the king's
judge[1].  From that day forth I feared the king, hitherto
unknown to me in his power, and his laws, and I put
hooks into my jaws[2].

A.D. 1379.

Again, another misfortune happened.  For that noble
knight, sir John Arundel, being sent forth against the land

---

[1] Anthony Wood, following the account given by Knighton, says:—
"On the third of the Cal. of May (1388), arose a grievous discord
among the scholars of Oxon, that is to say between the southern and
Welsh on the one part, and the northern scholars on the other, and in
very short time did it so much increase that the scholars for the most
part (after several had been slain) departed to their respective
counties."  And again, under the year 1389, he tells us of a second
outbreak of the rioting, in Lent, which was quelled by the intervention
of the duke of Gloucester.  "But," he continues, "you shall have
from a certain inquisition taken by a jury that was appointed on
purpose to take an account of the matter:—On Thursday in the fourth
week of Lent, 12 Rich. II. (which is this year), Thomas Speeke,
chaplain, and John Kirkby with a multitude of other malefactors,
appointing captains among them, rose up against the peace of the
king, and sought after all the Welshmen abiding and studying in
Oxford, shooting arrows after them in divers streets and lanes as they
went, crying out 'War, war, war, sle, sle, sle the Welsh doggys and
her whelpys, and ho so loketh out of his howse, he shall in good southe
be dead,' &c., and certain persons they slew and others they grievously
wounded, and some of the Welshmen who bowed their knees to abjure
the town, they the northern scholars led to the gates," and dismissed
them with certain indignities not to be repeated to ears polite.  The
inquisition further gives the names of the different halls which were
broken into, and of the Welsh scholars who were robbed of their
books and other chattels, including in some instances their harps.—
*Hist. and Antiqq. of the Univ. of Oxford* (ed. Gutch, 1792-6) i., 518.

[2] Ezek. xxix. 4; xxxviij. 4.

of France to subdue it, with the flower of the youth of the A.D. 1379.
country, had his fleet shattered alas! by an unhappy storm
on Saint Nicholas' eve (5th December), and perished[1]. The
cause of his mischance was not unrighteously found in the
taxes wrung from the clergy and the people.

Ever from the time of such levying of tribute, called tax,
do I remember the kingdom to have suffered misfortunes
either from internal slaughter or foreign treachery. Was
it not so when the earl of Pembroke, carrying with him A.D. 1372.
the tax levied to subdue France, was plundered with his
men near Rochelle, and carried captive into Spain? The
same befell king Edward, who, after taxing the clergy and
the people, strove to invade France with a mighty host;
but the winds were against him, and, though for six months
long he lay near the shore awaiting their favour, he
returned unprofitably with his army, as is told above in
this volume[2]. See what says the prophecy of Bridlington
against the tax:—

"While reigneth tax, large grace shall not abound;
So work begun shall foolish fall to ground."[3]

And thus alas! it is known to fall. Further, there fled A.D. 1385.
before the face of this king Richard that most perfect man,

[1] Sir John Arundel, of Lanherne, was in command of an expedition
in aid of the duke of Brittany, and repulsed the French fleet off the
coast of Cornwall. He was afterwards wrecked and drowned on the
Irish coast. Walsingham (i. 418–25) attributes the disaster to divine
vengeance for an outrage on a nunnery at Southampton. Arundel
appears to have been one of the fops of the period. In his ship
were fifty-two suits of clothes: "pro proprio corpore novos apparatus,
vel aureos vel auro textos."

[2] The passage in the "Polychronicon" here referred to, is as follows:
—"Eodem anno, rex Edwardus cum magno exercitu mare intravit,
ad removendum obsidionem de Rochell; sed ventus contrarius non
permisit eum longius a terra recedere. Quare aliquamdiu prope litus
maris commorans ventum prosperum expectavit; sed nondum venit.
Demum cum suis ad terram veniens, illico ventus ad partes oppositas
se convertit." Walsingham (i. 315) has nearly the same words.

[3] The prophecy of John of Bridlington is a political review of the
reign of Edward III., compiled in the form of an ancient text with

A.D. 1385. William Courtney, archbishop of Canterbury, for that he was ready to stand up against such tax; and, pursued on Thames by the same king, he fled for his life in the garb of a monk, and sought safety in the parts of Devon[1]. Yet did they who were the movers of this persecution by the king die an evil death, of whom we have heard above, to wit sir Simon Burley and others.

Thus far, good reader, set not in order of years such things as have been told; for what I saw and heard I stored up in my memory, rather with regard to the truth of the event than to the time when it took place.

A.D. 1394. In the year of our Lord 1394, on Whitsun-day (7th June), died that most gracious lady Ann, queen of England, at the

a recent commentary. The author was supposed to have been John, prior of Bridlington, who died early in the reign of Richard II. In some MSS. the work is ascribed to John Ergome; but who he was does not appear. It is dedicated to Humphrey de Bohun, earl of Hereford and constable of England, 1361–1372, and was probably written about the year 1370. Its popularity is shown by the frequency of quotations from it by the writers of the fifteenth century, among whom Adam of Usk is not the most backward. As a specimen of the work: the passage quoted above, which more correctly is "Dum multat taxa non fiet gratia laxa. Sic opus inceptum laxum patietur ineptum" (dist. iij. cap. 2), has this commentary—"*Dum multat taxa*, id est, dum recipit taxam et exactiones de regno, *gratia non fiet laxa* sibi et larga, sed deficiet, et sic *opus inceptum* et *laxum* quod fuit de captione regis Francie, quando nos habuimus inceptionem et latam viam ad conquerendum regnum Franciæ, *patietur ineptum*, id est, deficiet seu destruetur."—T. Wright, *Political Poems and Songs* (Rolls series), i. 183.

[1] William Courtenay, successively bishop of Hereford and London, and archbishop of Canterbury, was son of Hugh, earl of Devon. Walsingham, under the year 1385, tells us of the archbishop's opposition to a tax being imposed upon the clergy; but on this occasion the king acted with him as against the designs of the nobles upon the possessions of the church. Earlier in the year, however, there was a quarrel between the king and archbishop, according to Walsingham, "ob leves occasiones" (ij. 128), when the latter was threatened with deprivation of temporalities. The Monk of Evesham (57) gives as the cause of his disgrace the king's anger at his remonstrance against bad government, and adds that the archbishop had to hide himself. Has our chronicler confused the two events?

manor of Shene, which lies on Thames near to Brentford. A.D. 1394.
Which manor, though a royal one and very fair, did king
Richard, by reason that that lady's death happened therein,
command and cause to be utterly destroyed. After the
ceremony of her funeral, which was carried out with
becoming honours on the morrow of Saint Peter ad Vincula
(2nd August), the king, clad, with his train, in weeds
of mourning, straightway passed over into Ireland with
a great power, to subdue the rebellion of the Irish[1]. Yet
he gained but little; for the Irish, then feigning submission
to his will, straightway after his departure were in revolt,
as all men know.

The next year, at the end of May, the king returned to A.D. 1395.
England, landing at Bristol; and forthwith he sent envoys
into France to contract his second marriage, of which more
anon. And so, a matter for wonder, he took to wife a child A.D. 1396.
not yet seven years old, rejecting the daughter and heiress
of the king of Aragon, though very fair and of marriageable
years[2]. But why he chose this young child,—and though
a child she was married to him at Calais with much outlay
of money and show—they say was that, eager to pour forth
his pent-up venom, he thought by help and favour of the
king of France to destroy his enemies. Yet this in the
end turned to the ruin of himself and his confederates, as
will afterwards appear[3].

[1] Richard sailed for Ireland early in September, 1394, and returned
in May of the next year.

[2] The actual age of Isabella of France was eight years. The
marriage took place at Calais, on the 1st November, 1396. The
daughter of the king of Aragon, referred to above, appears to have
been Yolande, daughter of John I. She married, in 1400, Louis II.,
titular king of Naples and count of Provence, and thus became
grandmother to Margaret of Anjou, the wife of Henry VI.

[3] The surrender by Richard, in 1393 and 1397, of Cherbourg and
Brest, which were held in pawn of the king of Navarre and duke of
Brittany, was most distasteful to the English. Men recalled the
conquests of Edward III. and their speedy loss, and had come to look
upon even the giving up of towns held in pledge as a national wrong.
This, added to the French marriage, gave rise to various rumours of

A parliament was holden in London, at Westminster, on Saint Lambert's day (17th September), a Monday, in the year of our Lord 1397 ; in which parliament I, the writer of this chronicle, was present every day[1].

In the first place, a speech, in the form of a sermon[2], was made by Edmund Stafford, bishop of Exeter, then chancellor, wherein he kept his discourse to the one point: that the power of the king lay singly and wholly in the king, and that they who usurped or plotted against it were worthy of the penalties of the law. Wherefore, to this end was it ordained of parliament: first, to enquire after those who molest the power of the king and his royalty; secondly, what penalties such molesters shall receive; thirdly, that things be so ordered that henceforth such molesting do not ensue. And straightway the king bade the commons that then and there, before their departure, they agree upon a speaker, and present him on the morrow, at eight of the clock. The king also made proclaim his grace to all who might be among the aforesaid offenders, only excepting fifty[3] persons and certain others to be impeached in this parliament, provided that they sued out in effect their

Richard's designs in favour of the French: among others, that Calais, too, was to be handed over to them. See the story of Richard's quarrel, on this score, with the duke of Gloucester, as told in the *Chronique de la Traïson et Mort de Richart II.*, ed. B. Williams (English Hist. Soc.), 1846.

[1] It will be seen that the account of the proceedings of the parliament as given by our author is nearly the same as that found in the pages of the Monk of Evesham. One or two passages are given more correctly in this text. Whether the one copied from the other, or both from the same source, is not very material. But it is of importance to notice that Adam was present during the session, and that therefore the story which he tells may be looked upon as a true one.

[2] The text was from Ezekiel xxxvij. 22, "One king shall be king to them all."—*Rot. Parl.* iij. 347.

[3] By a confusion of the abbreviation of l. for *quinquaginta*, and r. for *vel*, Hearne, in his edition of the Monk of Evesham's Life of Richard, has erroneously printed *vel* in this place. Otterbourne has the correct reading.

letters of pardon before Saint Hilary.  He caused, too, proclamation to be made that no man henceforth carry arms of offence or defence in parliament, save only our lord the king's own retinue.

On the Tuesday (18th September), sir John Bushy [1] was by the commons presented to the king their speaker in parliament, he making first due declaration ; and the king accepted him.

Then straightway spake he thus before the king: " In that, my lord the king, we are bound by your dread command to make known to your royal highness who they be who transgressed against your majesty and royalty, we say that Thomas, duke of Gloucester, and Richard, earl of Arundel, did, in the tenth year of your reign, traitorously force you, by means of him who is now archbishop of Canterbury [2], and who was then chancellor, thereby doing you grievous wrongs, to grant to them a commission to govern your kingdom and to order its estate, to the prejudice of your majesty and royalty."

Also, the same day, that same commission was made of none effect, with all and every the acts thereon depending or thereby caused.

Also, a general pardon, granted after the great parliament by their means, and a special pardon granted to the earl of Arundel were recalled [3].  It was also prayed by the

---

[1] Bushy had been first elected speaker of the commons in 1394.

[2] Thomas Fitzalan, also called Arundel, was the third son of Richard, ninth earl of Arundel.  He had been made bishop of Ely, in 1374, when in his twenty-second year, was translated to York in 1388, and to Canterbury in 1396.  He was banished by the present parliament of 1397, and received from the pope translation to the see of St. Andrew's *in partibus infidelium*, the same appointment which had been conferred upon Alexander Nevill, his predecessor at York.  He was restored to Canterbury on Henry's accession, and lived to the year 1413.

[3] This special pardon had been granted to the earl of Arundel on the 30th of April, 1394, and was the more binding on Richard as it was granted at a time when he was his own master and entirely free from coercion.

commons, still by the mouth of their speaker, that, whereas that special pardon had been gotten for a traitor by Thomas Arundel, archbishop of Canterbury, then chancellor of England, he, the procurer of the same, who should rather by virtue of his office have been against it, should be declared a traitor. And the archbishop rose up, wishing to make answer; but the king said: "To-morrow." But thenceforth he appeared not there again. The king also said, as to this petition, that he would take counsel.

Also, it was decreed that any man henceforth convicted of acting against the government of our lord the king should be declared a false traitor, and the fitting punishment of treason be awarded to him. Also, it was decreed, with assent of the prelates, that criminal charges henceforth be determined without their agreement, in every parliament. And then having leave they withdrew.

Then there was, as is wont to be, some bustle. And thereupon the king's archers, who, to the number of four thousand, surrounded the parliament-house, which was set up to this end in the middle of the palace-yard [1], thought that some quarrel or strife had arisen in the house; and, bending their bows, they drew their arrows to the ear, to the great terror of all who were there; but the king quieted them [2].

On the Wednesday (19th September), the same statute of the prelates was repealed; and they were bidden, under pain of loss of temporalities, to the stablishing of what

---

[1] This parliament was held in a building specially set up for the purpose. "Fecerat autem rex ante istud parliamentum in medio palacii apud Westmonasterium, unam aulam inter turrim et hostium magnæ aulæ situatam, ad judicia sua ibidem exercenda. In qua gloriosius et solemnius sedebat quam unquam aliquis rex istius regni residere consuevit. Quam quidem aulam mox, finito parliamento, prosterni fecit et penitus inde asportari."—Mon. Evesh. 131. See also an account of the building in *Annales Ric. II.* printed with the chronicle of J. de Trokelowe, ed. H. T. Riley (Rolls series), 209; and in Otterbourne's Chronicle, 191.

[2] The Monk of Evesham (134) improves upon this account by adding that the archers began to shoot.

should be done in the same parliament, on that very day
to agree upon one who should be their attorney to consent
in their name to all that should be brought to pass in that
parliament.

The king also spake these words : " Sir John Bushy,
forasmuch as many ask me to disclose those fifty persons
who are excepted in the general pardon, I simply will not ;
and whosoever asks it is worthy of death [1]. First, because
they would flee ; secondly, because I have also excepted
those who shall be impeached in this parliament ; thirdly,
because, by naming them, others, their fellows, would fear,
when there should be no need for fear."

On the Thursday (20th September), my lord of Canterbury came to the palace on his way to parliament ; but the
king sent him word, by the bishop of Carlisle [2], that he
should withdraw to his lodging, which was done ; and
thenceforth he appeared not.

The prelates made sir Thomas Percy [3], the king's seneschal,
their attorney, with clauses of stipulations, to agree to all
that should be done in parliament.

Also, sir John Bushy spake as follows : " My lord the
king, forasmuch as the second article of this parliament
is concerning the pains to be laid on such as do violence
to your royalty, I beseech you that you deign to give me

---

[1] This sentence is given in the Monk of Evesham's work in a
mutilated form, from which no sense can be extracted.

[2] Thomas Merke.

[3] Thomas Percy, brother of Henry Percy, earl of Northumberland,
created earl of Worcester at the close of this session, 29th September,
1397. He was born about 1344, and served in the campaigns of
Edward's and Richard's reigns, both by land and sea. He became
seneschal of the household in 1393. He was admiral of the fleet for
Ireland in 1399, and accompanied the king thither, and returned with
him to Milford. By some of the chroniclers he is accused of having
then deserted to Henry ; at any rate he was present in the parliament
which approved Richard's deposition, and was taken into favour by
Henry. He joined the revolt of the Percys, and was beheaded after
the battle of Shrewsbury.

A.D. 1397. authority, by way of appeal, accusation, or impeachment, with leave to change from one to the other, as often as or whenever it shall unto me seem good and to my fellows." And so was it done. Then Bushy spake again : " I accuse Thomas Arundel, archbishop of Canterbury, of threefold treason. First, of the commission of government of your kingdom, treasonably granted to him, to Thomas, duke of Gloucester, and to Richard, earl of Arundel, at his instance and through him, who ought rather, by reason of his office, in that he was at that time your chancellor, to have withstood it. Secondly, that under veil of that traitorous commission, treacherously usurping the legal authority of your royalty, they did treasonably hold a solemn parliament to the prejudice of your royalty. Thirdly, that by such treacherous usurpation sir Simon de Burley and sir James Berners, knights and your faithful lieges, were traitorously done to death. Wherefore we, your commons, pray that a fitting judgement for so great treasons be by you issued against him. And seeing that the same archbishop is a man of great kindred, alliance, and wealth, and of a most cunning and cruel nature, I pray, for the salvation of your estate and of all your realm, as well as for the despatch of this present parliament, that he be set in safe keeping until the last fulfilment of his judgement." The king thereto answered that, on account of the high station of so great a person, he would consider till the morrow ; and he declared all others who were joined in the said commission to be faithful, loyal, and free from treason, and specially Alexander Nevill, late archbishop of York. And then my lord Edmund of Langley, duke of York, the king's uncle, and my lord William of Wykeham, bishop of Winchester, who had been of the commission, shedding tears, fell on their knees and thanked the king for so great favour.

Also on the Friday (21st September), which fell on Saint Matthew's day, the earls of Rutland, Kent, Huntingdon,

Nottingham, Somerset, and Salisbury, the lord Despencer, A.D. 1397. and sir William Scrope [1], in a suit of red robes of silk, banded with white silk and powdered with letters of gold, set forth the appeal which they had already proclaimed before the king at Nottingham; wherein they accused Thomas, duke of Gloucester, Richard, earl of Arundel, Thomas, earl of Warwick, and sir Thomas Mortimer, knight, of the aforesaid treasons, and also of armed revolt at Haringhay-park traitorously raised against the king. And, they having given surety to follow up their appeal, Richard, earl of Arundel, was put on his trial, clad in a robe of red with a hood of scarlet. And straightway the duke of Lancaster said to the lord Nevill: "Take off his belt and his hood"; and it was done. And when the articles of accusation were unfolded to the earl, he boldly declared that he was no traitor and claimed the benefit of his pardon granted aforetime, declaring that he would never withdraw him from the king's grace. But the duke of Lancaster said to him: "Traitor! that pardon is recalled." The earl answered: "Verily thou liest! never was I traitor!" Again the duke said: "Wherefore didst thou then get the pardon?" And the earl answered: "To close the mouths of mine enemies, of whom thou art one. And in truth, as for treasons, thou needest pardon more than I." Then said the king to him: "Answer to the appeal." The earl replied: "I see well that those persons accuse me of treason by showing appeals. In sooth they lie, all of them! Never was I traitor! I claim ever the benefit of my pardon, which, within six years last past,

[1] Edward Plantagenet, earl of Rutland, afterwards made duke of Albemarle or Aumarle, son of the duke of York; Thomas Holland, earl of Kent, afterwards duke of Surrey; John Holland, earl of Huntingdon, afterwards duke of Exeter; Thomas Mowbray, earl of Nottingham, afterwards duke of Norfolk; John Beaufort, earl of Somerset, afterwards marquess of Dorset; John de Montacute, earl of Salisbury; Thomas, baron Despencer, afterwards earl of Gloucester; and William le Scrope, afterwards earl of Wiltshire.

you, being of full age and of unfettered will, did of your own motion grant to me." Then said the king: "I granted it, saving it were not to my prejudice." Then said the duke of Lancaster: "So the grant holds not good." The earl replied: "Surely of that treason I knew no more than thou who wast then beyond seas." Then said sir John Bushy: "That pardon is recalled by the king, the lords and us, his faithful commons." The earl answered: "Where be those faithful commons? Well do I know thee and thy crew there, how ye are gathered together, not to do faithfully, for the faithful commons are not here. They, I know, are sore grieved for me; and I know that thou hast ever been false." And then Bushy and his fellows cried out: "See, my lord the king, how this traitor strives to stir up discord between us and the commons of the land who abide at home!" The earl answered: "Ye are all liars! I am no traitor!" Then rose up the earl of Derby and said to him: "Didst thou not say to me at Huntingdon, where first we were gathered to revolt, that it would be better first of all to seize the king?" The earl replied: "Thou, earl of Derby, thou liest at thy peril! Never had I thought concerning our lord the king, save what was to his welfare and honour." Then said the king to him: "Didst thou not say to me, at the time of thy parliament, in the bath behind the White Hall, that sir Simon Burley, my knight, was, for many reasons, worthy of death? And I answered thee that I knew no cause of death in him. And then thou and thy fellows did traitorously slay him." And then the duke of Lancaster passed sentence of death upon him in these words: "Richard, I, seneschal of England, do adjudge thee traitor, and I do by sentence and judgement condemn thee to be drawn, hanged, beheaded, and quartered, and thy lands, entailed and unentailed, to be forfeit."

Then the king, having regard for his noble birth, commanded him to be beheaded only. And there led him

away his foes, the earl of Kent, his own nephew, and others
who coveted his lands,—and who were afterwards cut off,
as will appear, by an evil death,—to the Tower Hill; and
there did they behead him[1]. And with his soul may I be
found worthy to rest in bliss!, for, assuredly, I doubt not
that he is gathered to the company of the saints. As to
his body, though it was then without honour laid in the
church of the Austin friars of London, yet now is it most
gloriously worshipped with deep reverence and with
abounding offerings of the people.

On the Saturday (22nd September), sir Thomas Mortimer
was vouched, under pain of banishment as a traitor, to
appear within six months, to stand his trial. And the
king said: "Perchance the earl of March will not be able
to take him; I will therefore wait until his capture be
certified." The which sir Thomas, thus banished, stayed
the time of his banishment in Scotland[2].

It was also declared that all benefices granted and transferred by such persons as had been, or should be, condemned
in this parliament, and all other grants whatsoever made
by them since the tenth year of the king, be recalled.

[1] Richard Fitzalan, earl of Arundel, was uncle to the young earl of
Kent, his sister Alice having married Thomas Holland, second earl
of Kent, lately deceased. The earl of Huntingdon is also said
to have been present at the execution, and with him the earl of
Nottingham, earl-marshal, the son-in-law of Arundel, though it seems
that at this time he was at Calais (see Walsingham, ij. 225; Wallon,
*Richard II.* ij. 456). However, the common belief that Nottingham
was there appears in some lines of *Richard the Redeles* (pass. III. 105,
106), a poem written by William Langland in the year 1399 (ed.
W. W. Skeat, Early Engl. Text Soc., 1873), wherein the story told by
Froissart (IV. c. 92), that the earl-marshal actually bandaged his
father-in-law's eyes, seems to be alluded to. Arundel was deservedly
a favourite with the people. He was one of the best sea-captains of
the day, as he proved by his victories in 1387 and 1388.

[2] It will be seen, on p. 165, that sir Thomas Mortimer is called the
uncle of the earl of March. If he was so, it must have been by an
illegitimate connection, as he is not recognized in the genealogy of
the family.

On the Monday next following (24th September), was read the declaration of the earl of Nottingham, then captain of Calais, in whose keeping had been the duke of Gloucester, that the same duke could not appear on his trial, for that he had died in his keeping; and at the prayer of the said appellants the same judgement was issued against him, as against the earl of Arundel.

Thomas, archbishop of Canterbury, also, after that his temporalities had been seized, was banished the kingdom.

On the Tuesday following (25th September), Rickhill [1], one of the judges of our lord the king, a native of Ireland, read divers confessions drawn up in writings touching the said treasons, declaring them to be the confessions of the said duke of Gloucester, put forth by him and written with his own hand.

Also, the county of Chester was raised to the honour of a duchy, and was augmented by the addition of the forfeited lands of the earl of Arundel. And the earl of Salisbury prayed for a writ of *scire facias* to be granted to him against the earl of March touching the lordship of Denbigh in Wales; and the king answered thereon that he would consider it [2].

Also, on the Wednesday next following (26th September), it was decreed that the lands of the said earl of Arundel, which were added to the said duchy of Chester, should enjoy its liberties in all things, saving that the Welsh inhabitants of those lands should still hold their ancient rights and customs.

It was likewise ordained that all who gave counsel, help, or favour to the children of those who had been, or should be, condemned in this parliament, should be punished with

[1] William Rickhill, puisne judge of the Common Pleas.

[2] On the attainder of Roger Mortimer, first earl of March, in 1330, the lordship of Denbigh was granted to William de Montacute, afterwards earl of Salisbury, but returned, in 1342, to Roger, second earl of March, on the reversal of the attainder.

the pains of treason.   And the parliament was adjourned
to the next Friday.

On that day (28th September), the king declared what
issue of the condemned should be debarred from their
estates, and from the councils and parliaments of the king:
to wit, heirs male, and all descending from them in the
male line for ever.

Also, the king appointed to the said archbishop of
Canterbury a term of six weeks to withdraw from the
kingdom.

Also, it was ordained that all the lords, spiritual and
temporal, should swear to observe unswervingly whatsoever
had been or should be done, decreed, or despatched in this
parliament; the prelates also hurling their censures from
this time forth upon such as should make opposition.

Also, the earl of Warwick was brought to trial; and his
hood was taken from him, and the appeal was read.   And
like a wretched old woman he made confession of all
contained therein, wailing and weeping and whining that he
had done all, traitor that he was; submitting himself in all
things to the king's grace, and bewailing that he had ever
been ally of the appellees.   And the king asked him by
whom he had been lured to them; and he answered, by
the duke of Gloucester and by the then abbot of St. Albans
and by a monk recluse of Westminster; and he kept
begging the king's grace.   And then, all as it were lamenting and seeking the royal favour for him, the king gave
him his life to pine away in perpetual prison without the
kingdom, his goods, moveable and immoveable—as in the
case of the earl of Arundel—being first seized.   And then
the king sent him to the Tower of London, and at length
ordered him to be taken to the castle of the Isle of Man,
to be held in the keeping of William Scrope, lord of that
island, a prisoner for life.

Also, on the Saturday (29th September), the king allowed
to the earl of Warwick one month to betake himself to the

A.D. 1397. said castle of Man. He also pretended to grant to him and his wife five hundred marks for the term of their lives; but he never paid them one penny, but took everything from them even to their shoe-latchets [1].

Also, to the earl of Salisbury was granted a writ of *scire facias* against the earl of March as touching the lordship of Denbigh, allowing grace of forty days to answer.

Also, it was ordained that debtors of the bridge of Rochester be distrained to the use of the said bridge [2].

Also, the king declared that, as to the foray of the Scots, rumoured abroad in this parliament, he would in council find a remedy.

Also, the earl of Derby was made duke of Hereford; the earl of Rutland, duke of Albemarle; the earl of Kent, duke of Surrey; the earl of Huntingdon, duke of Exeter; the earl of Nottingham, duke of Norfolk; the earl of Somerset, marquess of Dorset; the lord Despencer, earl of Gloucester; the lord Nevill, earl of Westmoreland; the lord Thomas Percy, earl of Worcester; and the lord William Scrope, earl of Wiltshire. And the parliament was prorogued to

---

[1] Thomas de Beauchamp, earl of Warwick, had been governor to the king on his accession. He was condemned in this parliament, for his share in the events of 1386-1388. The reference in the text to the abbot of St. Albans and the monk of Westminster can only be connected with the story of Gloucester's conspiracy, which is told in the *Chronique de la Traïson et Mort de Richart II.* as taking place in 1396, and in which John Moot, abbot of St. Albans, and John Worting, prior of Westminster, were implicated. Richard did not leave Warwick long in the Isle of Man, but brought him back to the Tower, whence he was set free by Henry. His wife was Margaret, daughter of William, baron Ferrers, of Groby. Their bad treatment is noticed in *Annales Ricardi II.* (Rolls series), 220: "Ibi constituit eum in carcere perpetuo conservari, promisso, tam sibi quam uxori suæ, victu honorifico de terris vel redditibus quondam eisdem pertinentibus, modo tamen forisfactis. Sed hanc sententiam postea non implevit penes comitem et comitissam, sed in magna protrahere miseria vitam permisit utrumque."

[2] Old Rochester bridge, formerly built of wood, was now replaced by one of stone.—*Rot. Parl.* iij. 354.

be dissolved at Shrewsbury, the quinzaine of Saint Hilary A D. 1397. next following.

On the Sunday (30th September), the king made a great feast on the breaking up of the parliament; and it was done as was ordained on the Friday concerning the censures and oaths. But, although this parliament was ratified by the oaths of the lords, by the censures of the church levelled against evil-doers, and by confirmation apostolic, Peter, bishop of Acqs [1], in the name of the pope, in like manner hurling forth censures, yet, like the image of Nebuchadnezzar, in the height of its vain-glory it fell with its supporters, and righteously, according to what has gone before, as will presently more fully appear. The example of Chosroes, of Belshazzar, of Antiochus, and of other tyrants who have oppressed their people [2].

And so the king continued the parliament at Shrewsbury A.D. 1398. (28th January) with such worldly pomp, as ear hath not heard neither hath it entered into the heart of man [3]. What unprofitable things to the kingdom and destructive that great trooping together of people, all armed as though for war, did bring about, the world might wonder at. And in this parliament, besides other things hurtful to his people and ruinous to the price of food, even for his victuals he paid naught. And there was then appealed of treason the lord [John] de Cobham, for that he had been one of the twelve commissioners of the kingdom. And he said to the king in his trial: "It is well known to you that you did command me to take upon me the burden of the commission and to receive the same?" The king answered: "Thou knowest well that I bade thee do so against my will." "Assuredly not!" said the lord Cobham.

---

[1] Pierre du Bois, bishop of Acqs, in the south of France, formerly canon of Bordeaux. An order to seize his goods appears in Rymer's *Fœdera*, 30th May, 1400.

[2] This sentence appears to be a note of examples to be enlarged upon at a future time.     [3] 1 Cor. ij. 9.

A.D. 1398. And the king made him to be adjudged traitor by the duke of Lancaster; yet granted he him his life to pine away in prison. Thereupon the duke said to him: "Give thanks to our lord the king for thy life." "Nay, verily," said he, "for the rather my life wearies me, because I thought to rejoice in eternal life sooner than I shall do[1]."

Then and there, too, the king wrung from the clergy a tenth and a half, and from the people a fifteenth and a half, and on every sack of wool five marks, and on every tun of wine five shillings, and on every pound's worth[2] of merchandise two shillings, for the term of his life, amid the secret curses of his people[3]. At length he sent the said lord Cobham into perpetual prison in the island of Jersey.

To this parliament was summoned and came that noble knight, the earl of March, lieutenant of Ireland, a youth of exceeding uprightness, who had no part nor share in such designs and wanton deeds of the king. Him the people received with joy and delight, going forth to meet him to the number of twenty thousand, clad in hoods of his colours, red and white, and hoping through him for deliverance from the grievous evil of such a king. But he bore himself wisely and with prudence; for the king and others who were only half-friends, envying his virtue, laid snares for him, seeking occasions of complaint against him. But he, as though he cared not for the turmoil among the people, feigned in the king's presence, pretending that his

---

[1] John de Cobham, third baron Cobham, was at this time an old man, between eighty and ninety years of age. He was recalled from banishment by Henry IV., and survived till 1409. His granddaughter Joan was the wife of sir John Oldcastle. Walsingham (*Ypodigma Neustriæ*, Rolls series, 379) refers to him as "vir grandævus, simplex, et rectus," and confirms what Adam says regarding his indifference to life: "Rex tamen, concessa seni, quam non optavit, venia, sive vita, misit eum ad insulam de Gerneseya in exilium."

[2] The MS. reads, "librata ponderis."

[3] The parliament granted Richard a tenth and a half and a fifteenth and a half, and the tax on wools, skins, and wool-fells for life.—*Rot. Parl.* iij. 368.

deeds were pleasing to him, although in very truth they displeased him much. Yet the king mistrusted, and being ever evil-minded against him, for that others dared it not, thought with his own hands to slay him. And, with others thereto sworn, the king did ever seek occasion to destroy him, excusing his evil purpose in that the earl had received in Ireland, some while after his banishment, sir Thomas Mortimer, a bold knight, his uncle, who had been banished by them and whom they sorely feared, and had also before his departure furnished him with money. And so in secret among themselves they doomed the earl, striving to find a time to destroy him, and boasting that they would share his lands amongst them. And to that end they sent into Ireland, as their lieutenant, to take him, my lord of Surrey before mentioned, his wife's brother[1], who hated him bitterly. But alas!, on Saint Margaret's day (20th July), near to Kells[2] in Ireland, while, too bold in his warlike valour, he had rashly outstripped his own troops, he fell by the accident of war into the hands of his enemies and was slain, to the great sorrow of the realm of England, and to the no small joy and delight of his rivals and adversaries[3].

[1] Roger Mortimer, earl of March, married Eleanor, sister of Thomas Holland, duke of Surrey.

[2] Kenlasoe. MS. The place meant is Kells, co. Kilkenny.

[3] The following is an extract from a chronicle of the founders of Wigmore abbey, which is printed in Dugdale's *Monasticon*, vj. 354. The adoption by the earl of the Irish dress is rather a curious fact:— "Iste Rogerus, juvenis probitate illius temporis præclarus, hastiludiis strenuus, in facescia gloriosus, in epulis dapsilis, in muneribus largus, in communione affabilis et jocosus, pulcritudine et forma coetaneos excellens, in ætatis suæ vicessimo anno locumtenens Hiberniæ præficitur: unde de et super castro et villa de Dynnebygh, cum Rosse et Ruwynnok pago adjacenti, per comitem Sarum, consilio, auxilio, et favore ducis Lancastriæ in eventum victoriæ idem sibi dominium captantis, in ultimo parliamento dicti regis Ricardi, apud Salopiam tento, contra eum causa mota, ad defensionem, milibus colore suo indutis stipatus, et ab omnibus aliis pagensibus, etiam expensis propriis, pro majore parte, in coloribus suis, scilicet rubeo et albo,

This is the genealogy of the same earl: Roger, son of Edmund, son of Roger, son of Edmund, son of Roger, first earl of March, [son of Edmund, son of Roger], son of Gwladus the Dark, daughter of Llewellyn, son of Jorwerth the Broken-nosed, prince of North Wales. (And so, through the British kings, the heathen gods, and the patriarchs to Adam.) Now let us return to Gwladus the Dark, whose mother was Joan, [natural] daughter of king John, son of Henry, son of the empress, daughter of Henry the first, son of William the Conqueror, son [of Robert, son] of Richard, son of Richard the Hardy, son of William Long-sword, son of Rollo, the first conqueror of Normandy.

Besides this noble descent from the kings of Britain, Italy, Troy, England, France, and Spain, see how flourished the royal race of the earls of March! The same Roger above mentioned was son of Philippa, countess of March, daughter of Lionel, duke of Clarence, second son of Edward the third[1], glorious king of England and France, son of Isabella, daughter and sole heir of Philip, king of France: and this, too, in both direct lines. Also, by another line, he was son of the said Philippa, daughter of Elizabeth, duchess of Clarence, daughter of William de Burgh, earl of Ulster, [son of John de Burgh] by Elizabeth, daughter of Joan of Acre, daughter of Edward the first, king of England and conqueror of Wales, by Eleanor, daughter of the

vestitis, magnis cum gloria et gaudio receptus, in emulorum et adversariorum confusionem non modicum advenit, et dictum dominum summaliter [sententialiter?] et diffinitive evicit.

"Iste Rogerus, vir licet bellicosus et inclitus, ac negotiis fortunatus, pulcherque et formosus, ut præmittitur, fuerit, nimis tamen lascivus et in divinis heu! remissus; consilioque juvenum, antiquorum rejecto, abductus, nimia animositate, immo verius ferocitate leonina, Leonelli nepoti satis innata, sed (proh dolor!) non regulata, irruendo excercitum præcedens, Hibernicali vestitus et equitatus apparatu, nec suos in succursum expectans, ac hostes invadens, apud Kenles in Hibernia per homines Obrinque invasus, belli eventu in anno Domini mcccxcviij. cecidit inde, quia hostibus ignotus, quam dolenter trucidatus."

[1] Third son. William of Hatfield was the second-born.

king of Spain, his first wife.  Also, by another line, he was son of the countess Philippa, daughter of the said duchess of Clarence, daughter of the said earl of Ulster by Matilda, daughter of Henry, earl of Lancaster, son of Edmund, son of the third Henry, king of England, by Eleanor, daughter of the count of Provence, who is buried in honour among the kings at Westminster.  Furthermore, take note concerning Edmund, now earl of March, son of the said Roger, being under age and in the ward of the king [1], born of Eleanor, niece of king Richard the second, daughter of [Thomas] earl of Kent, son of Joan, countess of Kent, daughter of Edmund, son of the said Edward the first by Margaret, daughter of the king of France, his second wife, who lies buried before the high altar in the church of the grey friars of London.

Now let us go back to the said empress (Matilda), who was daughter of [Matilda, daughter of] Margaret, queen of Scotland, daughter of Edward the exile, son of Edmund Ironside, son of Athelred, son of Edgar, son of Edmund, son of Edward, son of Alfred, son of Athelwulf, son of Athelbry3t [2], son of Aelmund, who was one of the five chieftains of England.  The which Athelbry3t fled before the face of Bry3thry3t [3] his foe into France, in the time of Charlemagne ; but, Bry3thry3t dying, he came again into England, and bravely subduing all the other chieftains of the land he brought England into one kingdom, and peacefully dwelt therein ; and now he lies at Winchester.

Now let us go back to Ralph Mortimer, the husband of Gwladus the Dark and son of Roger, son of Hugh, the founder of the abbey of Wigmore, son of Ralph Mortimer who first came with William the Conqueror into England.

---

[1] He was kept prisoner of state by Henry IV. till 1413.  As he came of age in 1412, the above note about him must have been written before that date.

[2] i. e. Ecgberht.

[3] Beorhtric, king of Wessex.

A.D. 1398. This Ralph, leaving his son Hugh in his lordship of Wigmore, went back into Normandy and there died.

Now I must not omit to say something concerning Edmund, the father of the said Roger. This Edmund, who, within the space of two years, by his abounding virtues as well as by his warlike energy and vigour, wherein he surpassed all other mortals of his day, did wonderfully bring all Ireland, being then in rebellion when he came to his lieutenancy, into unity and peace and under the dominion of England,—he, I say, presented me, who am now writing, to a studentship in laws at Oxford, with fitting endowment. But alas! at his house in Cork, in Ireland, on the day of Saint John the Evangelist (27th December), through that fate whereby all are laid low, he left the world bereft of his great nobility, long time before I would have had it so. And his bones lie in Wigmore abbey along with those of his wife Philippa, buried in front of the high altar[1]. Concerning them are these verses :—

"One wise and good and well-beloved beneath
This marble turns again to earth in death.
Edmund's pure body lies within this grave ;
But Christ from prisoning tomb his soul shall save."

And for Philippa,

"A noble countess here entomb'd doth lie,
In deeds of ample charity she strove ;
Though sprung from kings, the friend of poverty;
For ever may she live in heaven above !"[2]

Through this Philippa, daughter of Lionel, second-born prince of England, as is above said, the earldom of March, besides its royal lineage, which might, belike, reach to the

---

[1] The Mortimers were short-lived. Of the last four earls, Roger was born about 1327 and died in 1360, Edmund lived from 1351 to 1381, Roger from 1374 to 1398, and Edmund from 1391 to 1425.

[2] The Latin original of these lines is also given in the chronicle printed in Dugdale's *Monasticon*, vj. 353.

highest places of dignity, rejoices in the honours wherewith it is endowed in the lordships of Clare [co. Suffolk], Walsingham [co. Norfolk], Sudbury [co. Suffolk], Whaddon [co. Bucks.], Crambourn [co. Dorset], and Bardfield [co. Essex], in England; of Usk, Caerleon, and Trelleck [co. Monmouth], in Wales; and in the earldom of Ulster and lordship of Connaught, in Ireland; together with the several and numerous appurtenances belonging thereto.

Now return we to the parliament of Shrewsbury. During its session, the duke of Norfolk, who afterwards died in exile at Venice, laid snares of death against the duke of Lancaster as he came thither; which thing raised heavy storms of trouble. But the duke, forewarned by others, escaped the snare [1].

The king meanwhile, ever hastening to his fall, among other burdens that he heaped upon his kingdom, kept in his following four hundred unruly men of the county of Chester, very evil; and in all places they oppressed his subjects unpunished, and beat and robbed them. These men, whithersoever the king went, night and day, as if at war, kept watch in arms around him; everywhere committing adulteries, murders, and other evils without end.

---

[1] "For you, my noble lord of Lancaster,
　The honourable father to my foe,
　Once did I lay an ambush for your life,
　A trespass that doth vex my grieved soul;
　But, ere I last received the Sacrament,
　I did confess it, and exactly begg'd
　Your grace's pardon, and I hope I had it."

*Rich. II.*, act I. sc. i.

Such are the words which Shakespeare puts into Mowbray's mouth, closely following the account given by Holinshed. From what source the latter took the story of the ambush does not appear. That such a plot against the life of Lancaster had a real existence is not unlikely, considering the jealousy with which he had been regarded in his days of power; but that Norfolk had designs upon him so late as the parliament of Shrewsbury can hardly be true. He is said to have refused to attend the parliament in 1384, fearing a plot against him (Mon. Evesh. 57).

And to such a pass did the king cherish them that he would not deign to listen to any one who had complaint against them ; nay, rather he would disdain him as an enemy.   And this was a chief cause of his ruin [1].

In the same parliament, the duke of Hereford, son of the said duke of Lancaster, appealed the duke of Norfolk of treason.   Wherefore the king appointed to them the morrow of the Exaltation of the Holy Cross [2] next following to fight in that quarrel.   The duke of Hereford meanwhile, finding pledges, went whither he would.   But the duke of Norfolk

---

[1] The excesses of Richard's Cheshire guards are a common topic with the chroniclers.   The archers who surrounded the parliament-house in 1397, as above noticed, were men of Chester, who had been specially summoned by Richard to form his body-guard (Walsingham, ij. 224).   In the *Annales Ricardi II.*, they appear as "natura bestiales, qui parati erant ad omnem nequitiam perpetrandam ; ita ut export tanta surrexit eis insolentia, ut regem reputabant in socium, et alios, quanquam valentes et dominos, haberent in despectum.   Et hii non erant de generosis patriæ, sed tracti vel de rure, vel sutoria vel alia quavis arte; ut qui domi vix digni reputati fuerant detrahere calceos magistrorum, hic se reputabant pares et socios dominorum."   Interference of these favoured subjects of Richard in other matters besides soldiering is noticed in *Richard the Redeles*, iij. 317, wherein the remarks in the text above on the king's protection of them are repeated in very similar words:—

"For chyders of Chester were chose many daies
   To ben of conceill ffor causis þat in þe court hangid,
   And pledid pipoudris alle manere pleyntis.

·    ·    ·    ·    ·    ·    ·

They constrewed quarellis to quenche þe peple,
   And pletid with pollaxis and poyntis of swerdis,
   And at the dome-ȝevynge drowe out þe bladis,
   And lente men levere of her longe battis.
   They lacked alle vertues þat a juge shulde have ;
   For, er a tale were ytolde, þey wolde trie þe harmes,
   Without ony answere but ho his lyf hatid.
   And ho so pleyned to þe prince, þat pees shulde kepe,
   Of these mystirmen, medlers of wrongis,
   He was lyghtliche ylauȝte and yluggyd of many,
   And ymummyd on þe mouthe and manaced to þe deth."

[2] This day would fall on the 15th September; the 16th was the actual day appointed.

being delivered into custody at Windsor, his offices were given over to his other co-appellors, that is, the office of marshal of England to the duke of Surrey, and that of captain of Calais to the duke of Exeter; on account of which grants, by His righteous judgement, God did send between him and them great confusion of strife, according to what the prophecy says in the verse :—

"By the Judge of Heaven's decree
The wicked throng shall bursten be." [1]

And on the day of battle they both came in great state to the appointed place, which was fenced with a wet ditch. But the duke of Hereford appeared far more gloriously distinguished with diverse equipments of seven horses [2]. And, because the king had it by divination that the duke of Norfolk should then prevail, he rejoiced much, eagerly striving after the destruction of the duke of Hereford. But when they joined battle, it seemed to him that the duke of Hereford would prevail. And so the king ordered the combat to be stayed, laying perpetual exile on the duke of Norfolk, yet being minded, when he should find occasion, to restore him. But the duke of Hereford he banished the realm for ten years. The one died at Venice in exile; the other within a year came back in triumph to the kingdom, and, deposing him who had banished him, reigned therein with might.

In this year, the morrow of Saint Blaise (4th February), died the duke of Lancaster, and in the church of Saint Paul in London, nigh to the high altar, was with great honours buried.

In the parliament of Shrewsbury, the king got the whole power of the government to be given over to him and to

---

[1] Bridlington, dist. ij. cap. vj.
[2] The combatants made a great display of arms and trappings. Henry was assisted by armourers sent by the duke of Milan; Mowbray received his arms from Germany.—Froissart, iv. 63; *Archæologia*, xx. 102.

A.D. 1398. six others to be named by him for the term of his life, where and when he should please[1]. By means of which
A.D. 1399. commission he afterwards condemned the said duke of Hereford to perpetual exile, seizing all his goods. And he passed sentence against the memory of many who were dead. And at length, in an evil hour, he set out for Ireland (29th May) to subdue it, for, as will hereinafter be seen, his return to his own land was to his injury.

The coming out of exile of the said duke of Hereford, now by his father's death become duke of Lancaster, and so twice a duke, was according to the word of the prophecy of Bridlington where are the verses :—

" With scarce three hundred men the duke shall come
        again ;
    And Philip, false, shall flee, all reckless of the slain." [2]

This duke Henry, according to the prophecy of Merlin, was the eaglet, as being the son of John[3].   But, following

[1] The commission to which were deputed the powers of parliament, at the close of the session of Shrewsbury, consisted of twelve peers and six commoners.  Half of their number was empowered to act.—*Rot. Parl.* iij. 368.

[2] Dist. ij. cap. ij.

[3] An allusion to the emblem of St. John, the eagle.  The "pullus aquilæ" is however not to be found in the prophecy of Merlin, as given in Geoffrey of Monmouth, but in the "Prophetia Aquilæ," which often accompanies it in the MSS.  The following is found in MS. Reg. 15 C. xvj. f. 184:—"Post hæc dicetur per Britanniam rex est rex non est.  Post hæc eriget caput suum et regem se esse significabit multis fracturis sed nulla reparacione.  Post hæc erit tempus milvorum et quod quisque rapuerit pro suo habebit, et hoc septennis vigebit.  Ecce rapacitas et sanguinis effusio et furni multis comparabuntur ecclesiis et quod alius serit alius metet et vitæ miseri mors prevalebit et paucorum hominum integra manebit caritas et quod quisque pepigerit vespere mane violabitur.  Deinde ab austro veniet cum sole super ligneos equos et super spumantem inundacionem maris *pullus aquilæ* navigans in Britanniam et applicans tunc statim et aliam domum aquilæ siciens et cito aliam siciet."  Those who have read Mr. Webb's translation of Creton's metrical history of the deposition of Richard will recall the scene of the aged knight who, as he rides along by Creton's side, tells him how the king's ruin had been fore-

Bridlington, he was rightfully the dog[1], by reason of his A.D. 1399.
badge of a collar of linked greyhounds[2], and because he
came in the dog-days; and because he utterly drove out
from the kingdom the faithless harts, that is, the livery of
king Richard which was the hart.

told by Merlin, as he was prepared to prove out of book (*Archæologia*,
xx. 168, 374, and appx. IV.).

[1] Adam no doubt refers to the line in Bridlington (dist. ij. cap. vij.)—
"Cum canis intrabit, leo cum tauro volitabit,"
which is thus commented upon: "*Cum canis intrabit*, id est, cum illa
stella nociva in cœlo, quæ canis primus dicitur, oriatur cum sole,
quod est quando sol est in fine cancri in mense Julii in diebus canicu-
laribus," *etc.* The adaptation of prophecy could scarcely be carried
further than to dub a man "dog" because he works out his mission in
the dog-days.

[2] The greyhound has not been commonly recognized as among
Henry's badges. The better known ones were the antelope, the white
swan, and the fox's brush. Here, however, is the badge of the greyhound, so specifically named that there can be no doubt that Henry
made use of it. Richard's cognizance of the white hart may perhaps
have suggested his rival's use of the greyhound at this time, with the
significance pointed to in the text. In the Harleian MS. 1989, f. 381,
containing a chronicle (unfortunately very corrupt) compiled at
Chester, is also to be found a reference to this badge:—"Unde creditur
quod armigeri ducis Lancastriæ deferentes collistrigia quasi leporarii
ad destruendum insolenciam missæ bestiæ," *etc.* (*Traïson et Mort de
Richart II.*, 283.)

The identification of the greyhound as a badge of Henry Bolingbroke
may explain a passage in *Richard the Redeles* (ij. 113), which has
caused some trouble to editors:—

"But had þe good greehonde be not agreved,
But cherischid as a cheffeteyne and cheff of ȝoure lese,
Ȝe hadde had hertis ynowe at ȝoure wille to go and to ride."

Mr. Wright supposes John Beaufort, earl of Dorset, to be here meant,
the greyhound being the cognizance of his family (*Political Poems*,
Rolls series, i. 386). Professor Skeat proposes Ralph Nevill, earl of
Westmoreland. There can, however, be no question that Henry is
more likely to be pointed to as "chief of your leash," than the other
two comparatively unimportant nobles.

With reference to these types and badges, it is a curious coincidence
that in the will of Edmund Mortimer, third earl of March, quoted by
Dugdale (*Baronage*, i. 149), a saltcellar in the form of a dog is
bequeathed to his daughter; and to Henry, lord Percy, a little cup,
made like the body of a hart, with the head of an eagle.

A.D. 1399. This duke Henry returned from exile in company with Thomas, archbishop of Canterbury, and Thomas, earl of Arundel, the son, who for fear of his life had fled to him in France from the keeping of the duke of Exeter, king Richard's brother; and he landed on the twenty-eighth day of June [1] with scarce three hundred followers, as above said, at a deserted spot in the northern parts of the land. And there first came to his help the chief forester of his forest of Knaresborough, Robert Waterton [2], with two hundred foresters; and afterwards the earls of Westmoreland and Northumberland, and the lords Willoughby and Greystock; and, in short, within a few days he stood in triumph, with one hundred thousand fighting men at his back. And two days before the end of July he arrived at Bristol, and there he struck off the heads of sir William Scrope [3], the king's treasurer, and sir John Bushy and sir Henry Grene, knights, the king's most evil councillors and the chief fosterers of his malice. There was I, the writer of this chronicle, present with my lord of Canterbury late returned; and I, through favour, made peace between the duke and the lordship of Usk, the place of my birth, which he had determined to harry, on account of the resistance of the lady of that place, the king's niece, there ordered; and I also got sir Edward de Cherleton [4], then

[1] The date of Henry's landing is variously given in the chronicles.

[2] Robert Waterton, afterwards a knight and Henry's master of the horse, is in some of the chronicles placed among those who accompanied Henry from France. In the Sloane MS. 1776—containing a chronicle which partly follows the Monk of Evesham and partly the *Annales* (ed. Riley), and which is partly independent,—and also in the Harleian MS. 53, a version of the Brut chronicle, as well as in Wyntown (ix. 20, 2001), Waterton figures as Richard's gaoler at Pontefract.

[3] The earl of Wiltshire, who is seldom named in the chronicles by his chief title.

[4] Sir Edward de Cherleton married, as his first wife, Alianore, daughter of Thomas Holland, earl of Kent, Richard's half-brother, and widow of Roger Mortimer, fourth earl of March. He succeeded his

husband of that lady, to be taken into the duke's following ; and I caused all the people of Usk, who for the said
resistance had gathered at Monstarri[1], to their great joy to
return to their own homes.

At length the duke came to Hereford with his host, on
the second day of August, and lodged in the bishop's
palace; and on the morrow he moved towards Chester,
and passed the night in the priory of Leominster. The
next night he spent at Ludlow, in the king's castle, not
sparing the wine which was therein stored. At this place,
I, who am now writing, obtained from the duke and from
my lord of Canterbury the release of brother Thomas
Prestbury, master in theology, a man of my day at Oxford
and a monk of Shrewsbury, who was kept in prison by
king Richard, for that he had righteously preached certain
things against his follies ; and I also got him promotion to
the abbacy of his house[2]. Then, passing through Shrewsbury, the duke tarried there two days ; where he made proclamation that the host should march on Chester, but should
spare the people and the country, because by mediation
they had submitted themselves to him. Wherefore many
who coveted that land for plunder departed to their homes.
But little good did the proclamation do for the country, as
will be seen. The reasons why the duke decided to invade
that country were : because, abetting the king, as has been
said, it ceased not to molest the realm for the space of two
whole years with murders, adulteries, thefts, pillage, and
other unbearable wrongs ; and because it had risen up

brother as baron Cherleton and feudal lord of Powis, in 1401. He
was also a knight of the Garter.

[1] I cannot identify this place. The scribe has probably blundered.
Perhaps Trostrey, two miles north of Usk, is meant.

[2] Thomas de Prestbury received the royal assent to his election as
abbot of Shrewsbury on the 17th August, and had the temporalities
on the 7th September, 1399. He afterwards got into trouble again,
for he received a pardon from the king in 14 Hen. IV., and again,
when indicted for felony, in 3 Hen. V.—Dugdale, *Monasticon*, iij. 514.

against the said duke and against his coming, threatening to destroy him. Another cause was on account of the right of exemption of that country, wherein the inhabitants, however criminal elsewhere, and others entangled in debt or crime, were wont to be harboured, as in a nest of wickedness; so that the whole realm cried vengeance on them.

On the eighth [1] day of August, the duke with his host entered the county of Chester, and there, in the parish of Coddington and other neighbouring parishes, taking up his camping ground and pitching his tents, nor sparing meadow nor cornfield, pillaging all the country round, and keeping strict watch against the wiles of the men of Chester, he passed the night. And I, the writer of this chronicle, spent a not uncheerful night in the tent of the lord of Powis. Many in neighbouring places, drinking of the poisoned cups given to them by the people of Chester, perished. There also, from divers water-cisterns, which the men probed with spears, and from other hiding-places, vessels and much other goods were drawn forth and taken for plunder, I being present with the finders.

On the morrow, which was the eve of Saint Lawrence (9th August), I went in the morning to the church of Coddington, to celebrate mass; but I found nothing, for everything was carried off and doors and chests broken open.

On the same day the duke of Lancaster with his host reached Chester. But first he mustered his troops in a large and fair field, wherein was a crop of standing corn, some three miles from the city, on its eastern side, marshalling their ranks to the number of one hundred thousand fighting men. And it may be truly said that the hills shone again with their shields. And thus he entered the castle of Chester; and there he remained for twelve days, he and

[1] The MS. reads "nono"; but the date is rectified by the next paragraph.

his men, using king Richard's wine which was found there in good store, laying waste fields, pillaging houses, and, in short, taking as their own everything they wanted for use or food, or which in any way could be turned to account[1].

On the third day of his arrival there he caused the head of Perkin de Lye[2], who was reckoned a great evil-doer, to be struck off and fixed on a stake beyond the eastern gate. This Perkin, who as chief warden of the royal forest of Delamere[3], and by authority of that office, had oppressed and ground down the country people, was taken in a monk's garb; and because, as it was said, he had done many wrongs in such disguise, he deservedly passed away out of the world in that dress. One thing I know, that I thought no man grieved for his death.

King Richard, hearing in Ireland of the landing of the duke, set out in the full glory of war and wealth, and made for the shores of Wales at Pembroke with a great host, and landed on the day of Saint Mary Magdalene (22nd July), sending forward the lord Despencer[4] to stir up his men of Glamorgan to his help; but they obeyed him not. Dismayed by this news coming in from all sides, and acting on the advice of those who I think were traitors, and hoping to be relieved by the succour of the men of North Wales and Chester, he fled in panic at midnight with only a few followers to Caermarthen[5], on the road to Conway castle in North Wales. Whereupon the dukes, earls, barons, and all who were with him in his great host,

---

[1] See the *Traïson et Mort*, appendix C, 231.

[2] Sir Piers de Legh, of Lyme Hanley.

[3] The jurisdiction of the forest of Delamere was vested in four families: Kingsley, Grosvenor, Wever, and Merton.—Ormerod, *History of Cheshire* (1819), ij. 50.

[4] Thomas Despencer, created earl of Gloucester in 1397; beheaded in 1400.

[5] The Harl. MS. 1989, printed in the *Traïson et Mort*, appendix C, 282, also mentions Caermarthen as the place whither Richard first went on landing in Wales.

A.D. 1399. according to the text: "Smite the shepherd and the sheep shall be scattered,"[1] disbanded, and making their way through by-ways into England were robbed of everything by the country people[2]. And I saw many of the chief men come in to the duke thus stripped; and many of them, whom he trusted not, he delivered into divers keepings.

On the eve of the Assumption of the Blessed Virgin (14th August)[3], my lord of Canterbury and the earl of Northumberland went away to the king at the castle of Conway, to treat with him on the duke's behalf; and the king, on condition of saving his dignity, promised to surrender to the duke at the castle of Flint. And so, delivering up to them his two crowns, valued at one hundred thousand marks, with other countless treasure[4], he straightway set forth to Flint. There the duke coming to him with twenty thousand chosen men—the rest of his host being left behind to guard his quarters and the country and castle and city of Chester[5]—sought the king within the castle (for he

[1] Zech. xiij. 7.

[2] See *Archæologia*, xx. 104, 328, where Creton tells us how the English soldiers were pillaged by the Welsh as they made their way through the country.

[3] In the *Traïson et Mort*, 195, the earl of Northumberland receives his instructions on the 17th August. As, however, he was at Conway on the 18th of the month, and had to make his arrangements and post his troops, the date in our chronicle is probably the more correct one. Both Creton (*Arch.* xx.) and the author of the *Traïson et Mort* state that Northumberland alone was present at Conway, and that the archbishop met the king at Flint. Consequently, the truth of Richard's promise to abdicate, which, according to the Rolls of Parliament (iij. 416), was made at Conway to the archbishop and earl, is open to doubt. See *Traïson et Mort*, 202; Lingard, *Hist. Engl.*; Wallon, *Richard II.* ij. 292.

[4] This story of the surrender of treasure is not supported by other chronicles. Perhaps the capture of treasure at Holt castle, which surrendered to Henry, is meant.—*Arch.* xx. 122.

[5] Creton has drawn a fine scene in which Richard stands on the battlements of Flint castle and watches Henry's army advance and encircle the fortress (*Arch.* xx. 155, 370). The number of troops is put down at 100,000 men, and the whole body is represented as

would not come forth), girding it round with his armed men on the one side and with his archers on the other; whereby was fulfilled the prophecy: "The white king shall array his host in form of a shield." [1] And he led him away prisoner to Chester castle, where he delivered him into safe keeping. Thus, too, he placed in custody certain lords, taken along with the king, to be kept till the parliament which was to begin on the morrow of Michaelmas-day.

While the duke was then at Chester, three of the twenty-four aldermen of the city of London, on behalf of the same city, together with other fifty citizens, came to the duke, and recommended their city to him, under their common seal, renouncing their fealty to king Richard [2]. They told, too, how the citizens had gathered in arms to Westminster abbey to search for the king, hearing that he had in secret fled thither; and that, not finding him there, they had ordered to be kept in custody, till parliament, Roger Walden, Nicholas Slake, and Ralph Selby, the king's special councillors, whom they did find [3]. And so the duke, having gloriously, within fifty days, conquered both king and kingdom, marched to London; and there he placed the captive king in the Tower, under fitting guard.

marching to Flint. Dr. Lingard has made some allowance, and reduced the number to 80,000. Twenty thousand men would, however, be quite enough for Henry's purpose; and I have no doubt that Adam's account of the disposition of the troops is right.

[1] This comes from the "Prophetia Aquilæ":—" Exercitus ejus ad modum clipei formabuntur."—MS. Reg. 15 C. xvj.

[2] The deputation from London is also said to have met Henry at Lichfield (*Arch.* **xx.** 176), or at Coventry (*Traïson et Mort*, 212).

[3] Holinshed (ed. 1807, ij. 859) tells a somewhat similar story: that some of the Londoners designed to slay Richard on his arrival in the city, but, being prevented, "They, comminge to Westminster, tooke maister John Sclake, deane of the king's chappell, and from thence brought him to Newgate, and there laid him fast in irons." Roger Walden was shortly afterwards deposed from the archbishopric of Canterbury. Nicholas Slake was prebendary of York, and dean of the king's chapel, Westminster. Ralph de Selby had been subdean of York, and was warden of King's Hall, Cambridge.

A.D. 1399. Meanwhile the duke sent to Ireland for his eldest son Henry, and for Humphrey, son of the duke of Gloucester, who had been imprisoned in the castle of Trim by king Richard. And when they had been sent over to him, along with great treasure belonging to the king, the said Humphrey, having been poisoned in Ireland, as was said, by the lord Despencer, died, to the great grief of the land, on his coming to the isle of Anglesey in Wales[1]. But the duke's son came safe to his father, and brought with him in chains sir William Bagot[2], a knight of low degree, who had been raised by the king to high places.

It was of king Richard's nature to abase the noble and exalt the base, as of this same sir William and other low-born fellows he made great men, and of very many unlettered men he made bishops, who afterwards fell ruined by their irregular leap into power[3]. Wherefore of this king Richard, as of Arthgallo, once king of Britain, it may well be said in this wise: Arthgallo debased the noble and raised up the low, he took from every man his wealth, and gathered countless treasure; wherefore the chiefs of the land, unable longer to bear such great wrongs, revolting against him, put him aside and set up his brother to be king[4]. So in all things was it with king Richard; concerning whose birth much evil report was noised abroad,

---

[1] Creton represents him as arriving in England, and as having, along with the young earl of Arundel, the custody of Richard confided to him at Chester.—*Arch.* xx. 173, 375. He is also said to have died of plague, either at Chester or at Coventry.

[2] Bagot had escaped from Bristol. He was afterwards set at liberty, and died a few years later in retirement.—*Arch.* xx. 278.

[3] The appointments of Walden, archbishop of Canterbury, Merke, bishop of Carlisle, and Winchecumb, bishop of Worcester, are here pointed at.

[4] Adam is quoting, from memory, from Geoffrey of Monmouth: "Nobiles namque ubique laborabat deponere et ignobiles exaltare, divitibus quibusque sua auferre, infinitos thesauros accumulans. Quod heroes regni diutius ferre recusantes insurrexerunt in illum et a solio regio deposuerunt" (iij. 17).

as of one sprung not from a father of royal race, but from a mother given to slippery ways of life; to say nothing of much that I have heard [1].

Next, the matter of setting aside king Richard, and of choosing Henry, duke of Lancaster, in his stead, and how it was to be done and for what reasons, was judicially committed to be debated on by certain doctors, bishops, and others, of whom I, who am now noting down these things, was one. And it was found by us that perjuries, sacrileges, unnatural crimes, exactions from his subjects, reduction of his people to slavery, cowardice and weakness of rule—with all of which crimes king Richard was known to be tainted—were reasons enough for setting him aside, in accordance with the chapter: "Ad apostolicæ dignitatis," under the title: "De re judicata," in the Sextus [2]; and,

---

[1] See the account in the *Traïson et Mort*, 215, of Richard's reception by the Londoners with the cry: "Now are we well revenged of this wicked bastard, who has governed us so ill!" Froissart (iv. c. 77) gives shape to these rumours in an apocryphal dialogue between Richard and Henry in the Tower, when the former was said to have resigned the crown. Henry, upbraiding Richard, says: "Et tant que commune renommée court, par toute Angleterre et ailleurs, que vous ne fûtes oncques fils au prince de Galles, mais d'un clerc ou d'un chanoine; car j'ai oui dire à aucuns chevaliers qui furent de l'hôtel du prince mon oncle, que pourtant que le prince se sentoit méfait de mariage, car votre mère étoit cousine germaine au roi Edouard, et le commencoit à accueiller en grand' haine pourtant qu'il n'avoit point de génération, et si étoit sa commère deux fois des enfants qu'il avoit tenus sur le fonds qui furent à messire Thomas de Hollande, elle, qui bien savoit tenir le prince et qui conquis l'avoit en mariage par subtilité et cautelle, se douta que mon oncle le prince, par une diverse voie, ne se voulsist démarier; et fit tant qu'elle fut grosse et vous eut, et encore un autre devant vous. Du premier on ne scut que dire ni juger; mais de vous, pourtant que on a vu vos mœurs et conditions trop contraires et différentes aux vaillances et prouesses du prince, on dit et parole, en ce pays ci et ailleurs, que vous fûtes fils d'un clerc ou d'un chanoine. Car pour le temps que vous fûtes engendré et né à Bordeaux sur Gironde il y en avoit moult de jeunes et beaux en l'hôtel du prince."

[2] Liber sextus Decretalium, ii. tit. xiv. § ij. This was the decree of deposition passed at the council of Lyons, in 1245, by pope Innocent IV. against the emperor, Frederick II.

although he was ready himself to yield up the crown, yet for better security was it determined, for the aforesaid reasons, that he should be deposed by the authority of the clergy and people; for which purpose they were summoned.

On Saint Matthew's day (21st September), just two years after the beheading of the earl of Arundel, I, the writer of this history, was in the Tower, wherein king Richard was a prisoner, and I was present while he dined, and I marked his mood and bearing, having been taken thither for that very purpose by sir William Beauchamp[1]. And there and then the king discoursed sorrowfully in these words: "My God!, a wonderful land is this, and a fickle; which hath exiled, slain, destroyed, or ruined so many kings, rulers, and great men, and is ever tainted and toileth with strife and variance and envy"[2]; and then he recounted the histories and names of sufferers from the earliest habitation of the kingdom. Perceiving then the trouble of his mind, and how that none of his own men, nor such as were wont to serve him, but strangers who were but spies upon him, were appointed to his service, and musing on his ancient and wonted glory and on the fickle fortune of the world, I departed thence much moved at heart.

One day, in a council held by the said doctors, the point was raised by some, that by the right of descent from the person of Edmund, earl of Lancaster—they declaring that the same Edmund was the eldest son of king Henry the third, but that, on account of his mental weakness, his birthright had been set aside and his younger brother

---

[1] Sir William Beauchamp, distinguished as a soldier and sea-captain, became lord Bergavenny in 1392. He died in 1410.

[2] "For God's sake, let us sit upon the ground
And tell sad stories of the death of kings:
How some have been deposed; some slain in war;
Some haunted by the ghosts they have deposed;
Some poison'd by their wives; some sleeping kill'd;
All murder'd."　　Shakespeare, *Richard II*, act III. sc. ij.

A.D. 1399.

Edward preferred in his place—Richard's succession in the direct line was barred. As to this, see the history in the pedigree [1], known throughout England, that Edward was first-born son of king Henry, and that after him, and before Edmund, Margaret, who was afterwards queen of Scotland, was born to the same king. I have read the following in the chronicles of the friars preachers of London: "There was born Edward, eldest son of king Henry, at Westminster; whom the legate Otho baptized" (book vii. ch. xxv., A.D. 1239). Again: "King Henry gave to his eldest son Edward Gascony, Ireland, Wales, Chester, and Surrey" (book vii. ch. xxxvij., A.D. 1253). Again: "On the fifteenth day of May, in the battle of Lewes, the barons took prisoners king Henry and his eldest son Edward" (book vij. ch. xxxvij., A.D. 1253). Again: "Edward, eldest son of king Henry, went with his wife to the Holy Land" (book vij. ch. xxxvij., A.D. 1271).—*Polychronicon.* Again: "King Henry kept Christmas at Winchester. The same year of our Lord, 1239, was born to king Henry and queen Eleanor their eldest son Edward, on the seventeenth day of June." Again: "The king summoned the queen and his eldest son Edward into France, to treat of a marriage between him and the daughter of the king of Spain, in the year of our Lord 1254, and the thirty-eighth of king Henry." Again: "The same year was sent into Spain, in great state, the king's eldest son Edward, to king Alfonso, for the said marriage." —*Trivet.* Again: "Queen Eleanor brought forth her son Edward at Westminster, in the year of our Lord 1239."

---

[1] In the MS. the word is written "P. de Grw," as though it were a chronicler's name. The word "pedigree" is meant; and the common genealogical history of the kings of England, of which so many copies written on long vellum rolls are still extant, is referred to. Hearne prints from one of his MSS., at the end of his edition of *Robert of Gloucester*, a "petegreu" of the kings of England from William the Conqueror to Henry VI. The Harleian MS. 326 has the title: "Here begynnyt the peˆtegreu of þe kyng þat now ys." See Skeat, *Notes on English Etymology*, 209.

"Queen Eleanor brought forth her daughter Margaret, in
the year of our Lord 1241." "Queen Eleanor brought
forth her son Edmund, in the year of our Lord 1245."—
*Chronicle of Gloucester* [1].

On Saint Michael's day (29th September) there were sent
unto the king in the Tower, on behalf of the clergy, the
archbishop of York and the bishop of Hereford; on behalf
of the superior lords temporal, the earls of Northumberland
and Westmoreland; for the lower prelates, the abbot of
Westminster and the prior of Canterbury; for the barons,
the lords Berkeley and Burnell; for the lower clergy,
master Thomas Stow and John Borbach; and for the

---

[1] This passage is interesting, as it throws some light on the story of
the fabrication of a chronicle by John of Gaunt, with a view to make
out a claim to the crown by direct descent, and of the investigation of
the matter by the Privy Council. Hardyng is the author of the story,
and tells it in these words: "For as muche as many men have been
merred and yit stonde in grete erroure and controversy, holdyng
oppynyon frowarde howe that Edmonde, erle of Lancastre Leicestre
and Derby, wase the elder sonne of kynge Henry the thride, croukebacked, unable to have been kynge, for the whiche Edward his yonger
brother was made kynge be his assente, as somme men have alleged,
be an untrewe cronycle feyned in the tyme of kynge Richarde the
seconde be John of Gaunte, duke of Lancaster, to make Henry his
sonne kynge, when he sawe he myght not be chose for heyre apparaunt
to kynge Richarde. For I, John Hardynge, the maker of this booke,
herde the erle of Northumberlande that was slayne at Bramham More
in the time of king Henry the Fourth saie, howe the same king
Henry, upon Saynt Mathee daye, afore he wase made kinge, put forth
that ilke cronycle, claymynge his title to the crown be the seid
Edmonde, upon whiche all the cronycles of Westminstre and of all
our notable monasteries were hade in the counsell at Westmynstre,
and examyned amonge the lordes, and proved well be all theire
chronycles that the kinge Edwarde wase the older brother, and the
seide Edmonde the younger brother, and not croukebacked nother
maymed, but the semeliest person of Engelonde, except his brother
Edwarde. Wherfore that chronycle which kynge Henry so put furth
was adnulled and reproved" (ed. Ellis, 1812, p. 353). He goes on to
say that John of Gaunt forged the chronicle in consequence of the
parliament refusing to recognize him as heir to the throne after
Richard, and that he published it by placing copies in different
monasteries. See *Arch.* xx. 186.

commons of the realm, sir Thomas Grey and sir Thomas A.D. 1399.
Erpingham, knights, to receive the surrender of the crown
from king Richard[1]. And when this was done, on the
morrow, the said lords, on behalf of the whole parliament
and the clergy and the people of the realm, altogether
renounced their oath of allegiance, loyalty, submission,
service, and what obedience soever, and their fealty to
him, setting him aside, and holding him henceforth not for
king, but for a private person, sir Richard of Bordeaux,
a simple knight; having taken away his ring in token of
deposition and deprival, and bringing the same to the duke
of Lancaster, and delivering it to him in full parliament on
that day assembled. On the same day the archbishop of
York delivered first a discourse on the text: "I have put
my words in thy mouth"[2]; and then, having been made
by king Richard his mouthpiece, he, using the first person,
as though the king himself were speaking, read in full
parliament the surrender of his royal rank and the release
of all his lieges and subjects whomsoever from all submission, fealty, and homage, openly and publicly, as drawn
up in writings. And this surrender, the consent of all and
every in parliament being first called for, was openly and
distinctly accepted. Which being done, my lord archbishop
of Canterbury preached on the text: "A man shall reign
over my people,"[3] wherein he highly lauded the duke of
Lancaster and his strength and his understanding and his
virtues, exalting him, and deservedly, to be their king;
and, among other things, he spake of the shortcomings of
king Richard, and specially how he had most unjustly
stifled in prison his uncle, the duke of Gloucester, treacherously, and without a hearing or leave to answer; and how
he strove to overthrow the law of the land, to which he

---

[1] The Rolls of Parliament (iij. 416) also name sir William Thyrnynge
and sir John Markham, justices, and William de Feriby and Denis
Lopham, notaries.

[2] Is. lj. 16.                    [3] 1 Sam. ix. 17.

A.D. 1399. had sworn [1]. And so, in short, although he had sufficiently
made resignation, the sentence of his deposition, drawn up
in writing, by consent and authority of the whole parliament, was there openly, publicly, and solemnly read by
master John Trevaur of Powis, bishop of St. Asaph. And
so, the throne being vacant, by consent of the whole parliament, the said duke of Lancaster, being raised up to be
king, forthwith had enthronement at the hands of the said
archbishops, and, thus seated on the king's throne, he there
straightway openly and publicly read a certain declaration
in writing, wherein was set forth that he, seeing the
kingdom of England to be vacant, by lawful right of succession by descent from the body of king Henry the third,
did claim and take upon himself the crown as his by right [2];
and that, in virtue of such succession or conquest, he would
in no wise allow the state of the realm nor of any man to
suffer change in liberties, franchises, inheritances, or in any
other right or custom. And he fixed the day of his coronation for Saint Edward's day (13th October) [3] next coming.
And for that, through the deposing of Richard late king,
the parliament which was in his name assembled had
become extinct, therefore he ordained a new parliament in
his own name as new king, to begin, by consent of all, on
the morrow of the coronation [4]. He also thereupon made
public proclamation that, if any thought that he had claim
to do service or office in the coronation, by right of inheritance or custom, he should send in his petition, setting
forth the why and the wherefore, in writing, to the
seneschal of England, at Westminster, on the Saturday

[1] This sermon was not delivered by the archbishop till after he had
enthroned Henry.—*Rot. Parl.* iij. 423.

[2] Henry's challenge of the crown was made before his enthronement.—*Rot. Parl.* iij. 422.

[3] The Translation of St. Edward the Confessor.

[4] Henry's first parliament met before the coronation, on the 6th
October, and was then adjourned to the 14th October, the day after
the ceremony. It was dissolved on the 19th November.

next following, and that he should have right in all A.D. 1399. things.

On the eve of his coronation, in the Tower of London and in the presence of Richard late king, king Henry made forty-six new knights, amongst whom were his three sons [1], and also the earls of Arundel and Stafford, and the son and heir of the earl of Warwick; and with them and other nobles of the land he passed in great state to Westminster. And when the day of coronation was come (13th October), all the peers of the realm, robed finely in red and scarlet and ermine, came with great joy to the ceremony, my lord of Canterbury ordering all the service and duties thereof. In tho presence were borne four swords, whereof one was sheathed as a token of the augmentation of military honour, two were wrapped in red and bound round with golden bands to represent twofold mercy, and the fourth was naked and without a point, the emblem of the execution of justice without rancour [2]. The first sword the earl of Northumberland carried, the two covered ones the earls of Somerset and Warwick, and the sword of justice the king's eldest son, the prince of Wales; and the lord Latimer bore the sceptre, and the earl of Westmoreland the rod. And this they did as well in the coronation as at the banquet, always standing around the king. Before the king received the crown from my lord of Canterbury, I heard him swear to take heed to rule his people altogether in mercy and in truth. These were the officers in the coronation feast: The earl of Arundel was butler, the earl

---

[1] The MS. reads forty-two, instead of forty-six knights, and makes Henry knight four of his sons, in place of three. Holinshed gives the names of all the forty-six, who were created knights of the Bath. It is nowhere else said that Richard was present at the ceremony.

[2] This was the Curtana. The sword borne by the earl of Northumberland was the one which Henry wore on landing at Ravenspur, and was called the Lancaster sword. The earl did this service for the Isle of Man, which had been granted to him immediately on Henry's accession.

of Oxford held the ewer[1], and the lord Grey of Ruthin spread the cloths.

While the king was in the midst of the banquet, sir Thomas Dymock, knight, mounted in full armour on his destrier, and having his sword sheathed in black with a golden hilt, entered the hall, two others, likewise mounted on chargers, bearing before him a naked sword and a lance. And he caused proclamation to be made by a herald at the four sides of the hall that, if any man should say that his liege lord here present and king of England was not of right crowned king of England, he was ready to prove the contrary with his body, then and there, or when and wheresoever it might please the king. And the king said: "If need be, sir Thomas, I will in mine own person ease thee of this office."

This same sir Thomas had this service by reason of his manor of Scrivelsby, in the county of Lincoln, and so he held it by sentence and judgement, in the name of his mother, who was still living, the lady of that manor, as against sir Baldwin Frevyle, who claimed this office in right of his castle of Tamworth[2]. In this case I was counsel to sir Thomas, and I drew for him the following petition to serve as his libel: "Most gracious my lord seneschal of England, prayeth humbly Margaret Dymock, lady of the manor of Scrivelsby, that it please your noble lordship to grant to your said bedeswoman that she may, at the coronation of our most potent lord the king, do the service which belongeth to the said manor, by Thomas Dymock, her eldest son and heir, as proctor of the said Margaret in this matter, in form following: Prayeth Thomas Dymock, first-born son and heir of Margaret

---

[1] Holinshed says that sir Thomas Erpingham served the office of chamberlain, though it was claimed by the earl of Oxford.

[2] This was a son of the Baldwin who claimed the office at the coronation of Richard II. Both families claimed by descent from the house of Marmion.—Dugdale, *Baronage*, ij. 103.

Dymock, lady of the manor of Scrivelsby, before you, most
gracious lord seneschal of England, that you suffer him
to have the service belonging and due to the manor of
Scrivelsby in the coronation of every king of England;
which service sir John Dymock, father of the same Thomas
and husband of the said Margaret, and in right of the same
Margaret, did in the coronation of Richard, last king of
England; and in possession of which service the ancestors
of the same Margaret, lords of the said manor, have been
from the time of the Conquest till now: to wit, that the
king do make deliver to him one of the best chargers and
one of the best saddles of our lord the king, with armour
and ornaments and appurtenances of the same of full
equipment for horse and rider, just as the king himself
would be armed when going into mortal battle, to the end
that the same Thomas, mounted thus in arms on the same
charger, cause proclamation to be made four times within
the hall at the time of the banquet that, if any man shall
say that Henry, king of England that now is and his liege
lord, is not of right king, nor ought of right to be crowned
king of England, he, the same Thomas, is ready to prove
with his body, where and when and howsoever the
king shall think right, that that man lies. Prayeth also
the same Thomas the fees and rewards belonging to and
wont to be paid for this service when fully discharged,
to be to him rendered and delivered." [1] This rough
translation out of French into Latin does not pretend to
be exact; and so, reader, be lenient.

On this feast, a year past, had Richard late king forced
to depart the realm him who was on this same day crowned
king. Also, he had caused his parliament to be confirmed
at Westminster under pain of full censures by the mouth
of Peter du Bois, the pope's legate, and by his own
authority. And he had also threatened to destroy with

[1] A copy of the petition in French is to be found in Cotton MS.
Vespas. C. xiv. f. 137 b.

A.D. 1399. the last penalties the countess of Warwick, as she sued
for her husband who had been condemned, as told above;
and this he swore he would straightway do, were it not
out of consideration for her sex. On this same coronation-
day he had thought to crown his nephew, the earl of Kent,
at Dublin, with great worldly pomp, king of Ireland, and
had thought to sweep away in destruction many nobles
of the realm of England, who were to be craftily summoned
to that great ceremony, seeking to enrich with their
possessions the same earl and other young men whom, as
has been said, he had raised up. But this Richard, with
his youthful councillors, may well be likened to Rehoboam,
son of Solomon, who lost the kingdom of Israel because
he followed the advice of young men[1]. (i Kings xij.)

On the morrow of the coronation, which was the first day
of the new king's parliament[2], the commons presented to
the king their speaker, sir John Cheyne, knight[3]. The
king received liege homage from all the lords spiritual and
temporal. Also, the last parliament of the lord Richard,
then king, was declared altogether void. And this took
place on the Tuesday (14th October). On the Wednesday
the king promoted his eldest son Henry, by five symbols,
to wit, by delivery of a golden rod, by a kiss, by a belt, by

---

[1] "Thanne wolde right dome reule, if reson were amongis us,
That ich leode lokide what longid to his age,
And never for to passe more oo poynt fforþer,
To usurpe þe service þat to sages bilongith,
To become conselleris er þey kunne rede,
In schenshepe (ruin) of sovereynes and shame at þe last.
For it ffallith as wel to ffodis of xxiiij ȝeris,
Or yonge men of yistirday to ȝeve good redis,
As becometh a kow to hoppe in a cage!"

            *Rich. Redeles*, iij. 254.

[2] See above, p. 186, note 4.

[3] Sir John Cheyne had been ordained deacon when young, but
renounced his orders and became a Lollard and a companion of sir
John Oldcastle. For this reason the clergy were hostile to him. He
was accepted as speaker; but immediately resigned. John Doreward
was chosen in his place.—Wylie, *Henry the Fourth*, i. 51.

a ring, and by letters of creation, to be prince of Wales. A.D. 1399.
Also, the causes of the repeal of that parliament were
declared to be because of the fears of, and threats used
towards, the peers of the realm if they obeyed not the
king's will; secondly, because of the armed violence of the
king's supporters, which blazed forth in the parliament;
and thirdly, because the counties, cities, and boroughs had
not had free election in the choice of the members of the
commons. It was also declared that the parliament of the
eleventh year of king Richard, which was all the work
of the duke of Gloucester and the earl of Arundel, should
remain in full force. Also, that any one who had in any
way been deprived of his right by Richard's last parliament
should then and there be restored to his own. And the
king also granted and gave over to his eldest son the
principality of Wales, as well as the duchy of Cornwall,
along with the county of Chester.

John Halle, servant of the duke of Norfolk, because he
was present at, and consenting to, the death of the duke
of Gloucester, being condemned by parliament, is drawn,
hanged, his bowels taken out and burned before him, and
while still living is beheaded and quartered; and the
quarter belonging to the right arm is set up on a stake
beyond London-bridge.

At the time of this parliament, two of the king's servants
dining in London found in five eggs with which they were
served the distinct face of a man, exact in every respect,
and having the white in place of hair standing clear of the
face above the forehead and coming down the cheeks to
the chin; and I saw one of them.

The lord Richard, late king, after his deposition, was
carried away on the Thames [1], in the silence of dark midnight, weeping and loudly lamenting that he had ever been

---

[1] He was taken from the Tower, on the 28th October, to Gravesend
and removed thence in the disguise of a forester, to Leeds castle,
in Kent, and eventually to Pontefract.

A.D. 1399. born. And a certain knight there present said to him: "Remember that thou, in like manner, didst entreat the earl of Arundel in all things most spitefully."

My lord of Canterbury having come back from banishment, and having been restored to his church as against Roger Walden, prayed of the parliament leave to distrain the goods of the same Roger, wherever found, on account of the profits and other his goods received by Roger during the time of my lord's banishment, and so to exact and abate what was due to him; and it was granted. And it is true that the lord Richard had given to the same Roger all the furniture and other the household goods of the same Thomas, archbishop of Canterbury, as being confiscated, as he declared, even to the value of six thousand marks, besides the stock of the manors of the church of Canterbury; which goods the said Roger Walden, being raised to the archbishopric, did hold and enjoy. And of them the earl of Somerset, when the news came of the landing of the said Thomas in the kingdom, seized six cart-loads from the hands of Walden's servants, which he had sent off to Saltwood castle for safety, and afterwards delivered all to the said Thomas. And with regard to this, among other things, on the feast of the Nativity of the Blessed Virgin (8th September), short time before this parliament, while I was dining with my said lord after his return at Lambeth, I saw how the said Roger had taken away and stripped off from the ornaments of halls and chambers, which belonged to my said lord Thomas, but which had been turned into his booty, the arms of my said lord, to wit, those of the earldom of Arundel with a bordure, which he bore as son of the noble earl, and had set up and had sewed over them, in their stead, his own arms: gules, a bend azure and a martlet or [1]. However, they lasted not long; for, taking them down, my lord Thomas again restored his own arms

---

[1] An impression of Walden's seal with this bearing is preserved in Westminster abbey.

and badges by the skill of the weaver's handiwork. And
the arms of the said Roger, thus taken down, as I have
said, I saw lying under the benches, a laughing-stock, and
cast and flung out of window by the servants. I was
likewise a witness when the same Roger came to the palace
of my lord bishop of London to seek grace from the duke,
now king, and from my said lord Thomas; which, as far
as his life went, he found. And so Thomas and Roger,
if I may say so, were two archbishops in one church, like
to two heads on one body; that is to say, Roger, then in
possession by right, by the pope's authority, and my lord
Thomas, because he was not yet restored by the pope, in
possession in fact, by means of the secular arm, which
was all-powerful, because before him alone was borne
everywhere the cross of Canterbury, which had been given
up to him by the said Roger. This Roger was a modest
man, pious and courteous, in speech of profitable and well-
chosen words, better versed in things of the camp and the
world than of the church or the study. First, he was king
Richard's French treasurer (at Calais), then his secretary,
and at length treasurer of England and the king's chief
councillor [1]. Him the town of Walden in Essex saw
exalted from a butcher's son to the said honours, although
by a too hasty leap. Whence is fulfilled the proverb:
" Quick gains are soon lost "; and, again: " No man was
ever great all at once." And hence the verses:—

" When the grave shall be uncovered, bishop Thomas shall
        be gone,
    And upon the earth, uprooted, falls the once exalted
        stone."

" When the grave shall be uncovered ": that is, because
king Richard had it without ceasing in his sleep that the
head of the earl of Arundel was restored to his body;

---

[1] Walden was afterwards restored to favour, and became bishop of
London in 1404. He died in 1406.

A.D. 1399. wherefore he caused the tomb to be opened[1]. "Bishop Thomas shall be gone": that is, the banishment of the same Thomas. "And upon the earth," etc.: that is, Walden; which signifies the setting up of stones. And this is an ancient prophecy.

The commons prayed of the king, in full parliament, that he would make grants undeservedly to no man, and specially of such things as belonged to the crown. And thereupon the bishop of St. Asaph[2] burst out in these words: "This petition is unmannerly and unjust, in that it argueth for niggardliness in the king, a thing which is contrary to all royalty, whereunto the bounty of an open hand is the rather thought to be seemly. It argueth too that subjects may fetter their king in his own inborn goodness. Which things seem to me unworthy. Therefore let not the king, who giveth, but let him who seeketh unjustly or unworthily rather be punished." And this answer pleased me, according to the passage in the codex of Justinian: "De petitionibus bonorum sublatis."[3]

It was also ordained that the lords of the realm henceforth give not their suit or livery of clothes or badges, or more especially of hoods, to any man, except their own servants who are always with them, by reason of the many strifes which had been thereby caused in the realm.

Also, although all those who had been condemned in the last parliament of king Richard had of pure right been restored to their own, yet it was not so with the earl of Warwick, except by special grace, for that he had confessed that he had traitorously risen up against the king with the duke of Gloucester and the earl of Arundel.

Also, the king removed the body of the duke of Gloucester from the distant place on the south side of the church, where, in dishonour, Richard had caused it to be buried apart from the kings, and laid it with great pomp in the

---

[1] See Wals. ij. 226; *Annales Ricardi II.* 219.
[2] John Trevaur.          [3] Codex, x. tit. xij. l. ij.

place which the duke had got ready in his life-time, A.D. 1399. between the shrine of Saint Edward and the tombs of his parents, by the side of his wife who had died a short time before[1]. And there and then I heard a good sermon on the text: "Remember the end,"[2] which the preacher divided into three parts: firstly, remember thy life; secondly, thy stewardship; thirdly, thine end. Again, the first he divided into three: remember thy life, in its beginning, in its course, in its departure. So likewise the second: how thou hast entered upon the stewardship, how thou hast got, and how thou hast spent. So too the third: remember thine end, how thou shalt be summoned to judgement, how thou shalt be tried, and how thou shalt be judged. And then ended the parliament.

In these days my said lord of Canterbury bestowed upon me the goodly church of Kemsing along with its chapel of Seal, in Kent, and the goodly prebend of Llandogo, in the collegiate church of Abergwili. And the church of Shire-Newton, in Nether Gwent, which by indulgence of the see apostolic I had held with other cures, I got to be given to my cousin-german sir Thomas ap Adam ap William of Weloc, and his church of Panteg to another cousin, sir Matthew ap Hoel: to be held by them severally.

I also got, by great good fortune, for sir James de Berkeley, lord of Raglan[3], and for his wife Elizabeth and his heirs, under the king's great seal, the confirmation of that and other their lordships.

[1] "Thomas of Woodstock was interred on the south side of the Confessor's chapel, beneath the pavement, under a splendid brass (see Sandford, p. 230), of which nothing but the indentations can now be traced. His widow lies in the chapel of St. Edmund, under a brass representing her in her conventual dress as a nun of Barking."—Stanley, *Memorials of Westm. Abbey* (1868), p. 145, note.

[2] Ecclus. vij. 36.

[3] Sir James Berkeley, younger brother of Thomas, baron Berkeley, married Elizabeth, daughter of sir John Bloet, with whom he had the town and castle of Raglan. Dugdale notices the confirmation.—*Baronage*, i. 361.

Then, too, I saw with king Henry a greyhound of wonderful nature, which, on the death of his master the earl of Kent, found its way by its own instinct to king Richard, whom it had never before seen and who was then in distant parts; and whithersoever the king went, and wheresoever he stood or lay down, it was ever by his side, with grim and lion-like face, until the same king, as is before told, fled at midnight by stealth and in craven fear from his army; and then, deserting him, and again led by instinct and by itself and with no guide, it came straight from Caermarthen to Shrewsbury to the duke of Lancaster, now king, who lay at that time in the monastery with his army, and, as I looked on, it crouched before him, whom it had never before seen, with a submissive but bright and pleased aspect. And when the duke had heard of its qualities, believing that thereby his good fortune was foretold, he welcomed the hound right willingly and with joy, and he let it sleep upon his bed. And after the setting aside of king Richard, when it was brought to him, it cared not to regard him at all other than as a private man whom it knew not; which the deposed king took sorely to heart[1].

---

[1] By a remarkable coincidence Froissart tells the story of the greyhound, though in a different form. He lays the scene at Flint, at the moment when Henry and Richard are preparing to leave: "Entretenant que on selloit et appareilloit les chevaux, le roi Richard et le comte (Henri de Lancastre) devisoient l'un à l'autre de paroles, et étoient moult fort regardés d'aucuns Londriens qui là étoient; et avint une chose dont je fus informé que je vous dirai. Le roi Richard avoit un lévrier, lequel on nommoit Math, très-beau lévrier outre mesure; et ne vouloit ce chien connoitre nul homme fors le roi; et quand le roi devoit chevaucher, cil qui l'avoit en garde le laissoit aller, et ce lévrier venoit tantôt devers le roi festoyer et lui mettoit ses deux pieds sur les épaules. Et adonc advint que le roi et le comte Derby parlant ensemble en-mi la place de la cour du dit chastel et leurs chevaux tous sellés, car tantôt ils devoient monter, ce lévrier nommé Math, qui coutumier étoit de faire au roi ce que dit est, laissa le roi et s'en vint au duc de Lancastre, et lui fit toutes les contenances telles que endevant il faisoit au roi, et lui assist les

In these days was born at Usk a calf which had two A.D. 1399.
tails, two heads, four eyes and four ears. Such another
monster saw I also in my youth in the parish of Llancayo,
in the house of a certain woman, Llugu daughter of Watkyn
by name. There was born too, in the parish of Llanbatock,
a boy with one eye only, placed in his forehead.

On the eve of the Epiphany (5th January), the earls of A.D. 1400.
Kent and Huntingdon and Salisbury thought to slay the
new king by craft and fraud, and to bring back the deposed
king out of prison, for that they had lost their rank as
dukes and the possessions of condemned persons which had
been given to them [1]. And their chief design was against
the castle of Windsor, privily, with a great power of armed
men, feigning to hold a tourney there, and so seizing the
entrance they would have slaughtered the king and his
sons, and others, his body-servants. But the king, forewarned, suddenly hastened to London for safety. Wherefore the earls of Kent and Salisbury, on their way to the
county of Chester, to get the favour and help of those who
rose in their cause, passed through Cirencester; and there,
on the morrow of the Epiphany, they were beheaded in

---

deux pieds sur le col, et le commença grandement à conjouir. Le
duc de Lancastre, qui point ne connoissoit le lévrier, demanda au
roi : 'Et que veut ce lévrier faire ?'—'Cousin,' ce dit le roi, 'ce vous
est grand' signifiance et à moi petite.'—'Comment,' dit le duc, 'l'en-
tendez-vous ?'—'Je l'entends,' dit le roi, 'le lévrier vous festoie et
recueille aujourd'hui comme roi d'Angleterre que vous serez, et j'en
serai déposé; et le lévrier en a connoissance naturelle; si le tenez
de-lez vous, car il vous suivra et il m'éloignera.' Le duc de Lancastre
entendit bien celle parole et conjouit le lévrier, lequel oncques depuis
ne voulut suivre Richard de Bordeaux, mais le duc de Lancastre ;
et ce virent et sçurent plus de trente mille."—Froissart, iv. 75. See
Wallon, *Richard II.* ij. 488.

[1] Thomas Holland, earl of Kent, was degraded from his dukedom
of Surrey, and John Holland, earl of Huntingdon, from his dukedom
of Exeter, by Henry's first parliament. John de Montacute, earl of
Salisbury, did not hold a dukedom. The third peer who was thus
degraded was Edward Plantagenet, earl of Rutland, who had been
made duke of Albemarle.

A.D. 1400. a rising of the country people[1]. And many who were found with them were led away to Oxford and were there beheaded; whose bodies, quartered after the manner of the flesh of beasts taken in the chase, partly in sacks and partly slung on poles between men's shoulders, I saw carried to London and afterwards salted[2]. The earl of Huntingdon also, trying to escape through Essex into France, was taken by the country people, and, in the very place where the duke of Gloucester had yielded himself to Richard late king, he was beheaded by clowns and workmen[3]. Regarding which things the king wrote to my lord of Canterbury; who thereupon, taking for his text the words: "Behold, I bring you good tidings of great joy,"[4] made known the news to the clergy and the people of London, in the form of a sermon; and then, a "Te Deum" being sung, giving thanks to God he passed in solemn procession through the city.

Afterwards, many others, amongst whom were master Richard Maudeleyn and William Feriby, clerks, and sir Thomas Shelley and sir Bernard Brocas[5], knights, were drawn and hanged, and, as having knowledge of and as furtherers of this crime, were lastly beheaded.

And now those in whom Richard, late king, did put his trust for help were fallen. And when he heard thereof, he

[1] They were attacked by the townspeople in the house in which they had taken refuge, and were forced to surrender. This was on the 7th January. They were actually beheaded on the next day.—See Wylie, *Henry the Fourth*, i. 99.

[2] See the *Traïson et Mort*, 246.

[3] See Wallon, *Richard II.* ij. 517. Huntingdon was caught by the country people and taken to Chelmsford, whence he was sent to Pleshy by Joan de Bohun, countess of Hereford, one of whose daughters had married the duke of Gloucester, while the other was the first wife of Henry IV. She gave up her prisoner to the people, who struck off his head on the 15th January.—Wylie, i. 101.

[4] Luke ij. 10.

[5] Sir Thomas Shelley, of Aylesbury, was a follower of the earl of Huntingdon. Sir Bernard Brocas is wrongly named Barnabas in the MS.

grieved more sorely and mourned even to death, which A.D. 1400.
came to him most miserably on the last day of February,
as he lay in chains in the castle of Pontefract, tormented
by sir [Thomas] Swinford with starving fare [1].

[1] This is the only chronicle in which any of Richard's keepers is
accused by name of having taken a personal part in starving his
prisoner. The MS. reads " N. Swinford," Adam not knowing Swinford's
Christian name, and therefore writing " N." according to common
practice. Sir Thomas Swinford, afterwards captain of Calais, is meant,
for he is known to have had the custody of Richard (*Traison et Mort*,
lviij.; Wyntown, ed. Laing, ix. 20, ll. 2001-10). Of the different
theories of Richard's death, that, which is supported by our chronicle,
of gradual starvation by his keepers seems to be the most probable.
The question has been so fully discussed elsewhere, that it would be
superfluous in this place to repeat what has been so often told before.
As, however, Adam of Usk is a fresh authority, and an important
authority as being a contemporary, for the theory of enforced starvation, it may be well to see what the other early chronicles say on
this point. Walsingham tells us that on hearing of the death of his
friends Richard voluntarily abstained from food. The continuator
of the Croyland chronicle has the same story, which is also found in
various MSS., such as Cotton MSS. Nero A. vj. and Galba E. vij. The
*Annales Ricardi II.* (Rolls series) and Otterbourne follow this account,
but add that after abstaining some time Richard was prevailed on
to try to take food, but that it was too late as he could not swallow.
The Monk of Evesham gives the account of voluntary abstention,
but adds an important passage : "Aliter tamen dicitur et verius,
quod ibidem fame miserabiliter interiit." Similarly, the Sloane MS.
1776 has an alternative : "Rex Ricardus primo de Turre ad Leedes
infra Canciam, sub custodia Johannis Pelham ibidem; deinde ad
castrum de Pomfrete, ubi Robertus Watyrton fuerat custos, occulte
deductus est, ubi non habuit spem alicujus relevaminis. Et eciam,
pre nimia amicorum suorum interempcione, dolore, tristicia areptus,
non valuit consolari ; nec consolatorem habens, diem clausit extre-
mum, videlicet in festo sancti Valentini. Et qualiter, penitus a nobis
nescitur. Quidam tamen opinantur quod fame miserabiliter ibidem
interiit ; hoc est, quod privabatur penitus ab omni sustentacione
naturali, usque ad diem sue resolucionis." The Kirkstall chronicle,
Cotton MS. Domitian xij., has : "Postmodo Ricardus quondam rex
translatus est de turri Londonie usque ad castrum de Pomfret, ubi,
diu ante mortem pane et aqua ut dicebatur sustentatus, tandem fame
necatus est, secundum communem famam," in which account it
agrees with Harl. MS. 3600, a copy of Higden's *Polychronicon* with
continuation. In other MSS. we find more particulars of the duration

At the coronation of this lord three ensigns of royalty foreshadowed for him three misfortunes. First, in the procession he lost one of the coronation shoes; whence, in the first place, the commons who rose up against him hated

of Richard's sufferings. The chronicle of Peter de Ickham, in Harl. MS. 4323, states that, on his removal to Pontefract, "per tempus certum custodiebatur," and then, "tandem a cibo et potu per quatuor aut quinque dies restrictus, famis inedia, cum xxij. annis regnasset, expiravit." The same version appears in the chronicles in Cotton MS. Domitian iv., and Harl. MS. 3906, and again in many copies of the English chronicle of the Brut. All these authorities are of value, for, although it cannot be said that they are all contemporary, they are at least early and sufficiently near the time to show that, from the first, rumours of Richard's starvation were very generally believed. Of a later period is the chronicle in Cotton MS. Titus D. x., of the early sixteenth century, which has a more embellished account: that Richard, "ductus de loco in locum, tandem, ut opinio est vulgi, apud Pontifractum cibi inedia interiit. Nam dicitur cibaria in singulos dies, more regio, sibi apposita fuisse, sed esurienti non licuisse degustare." This appears in an English dress in Harl. MS. 53, a version of the Brut chronicle: "In the first yere of the regne of kyng Henry the iiijte, kyng Richard, which that was put doune of his rialte, was in the castell of Pountfret under the ward of sir Robert of Watirton, knyght, and there he was ich day servet as a kynge aught to be that he myght se it, but he myght come to non therof. Wherfore sone aftir he deyd for honger in prison in the same castell, and so he made his ende." Holinshed has printed this account, along with others, of the death of Richard. (For the various discussions on this subject, see *Arch.* vol. xx.; Tytler, *History of Scotland,* vol. iij.; *Traïson et Mort de Richart II.,* Introduction; and Wallon, *Richard II.,* vol. ij.)

The date of Richard's death is put by Adam of Usk rather later than in most of the chronicles. The 14th February is the usually received date. Richard was apparently supposed in France to have been dead as early as the end of January, a deed of Charles VI., dated on the 29th of that month, referring to him as "feu nostre tres chier et tres amé fils Richard" (Rymer, *Fœdera*). That such rumours were current in England is proved by the well-known minute of the Privy Council to which attention was first drawn by sir Harris Nicolas. The date of the council at which this minute was passed has been fixed between the 2nd and the 8th February, and the wording of the original memorandum to which the minute serves as an answer implies, although it does not express, an uncertainty as to whether Richard was actually then living. He was certainly dead by the 17th February, on which date payment was ordered (Pell Issue Rolls)

A.D. 1400.

him ever after all his life long: secondly, one of the golden
spurs fell off; whence, in the second place, the soldiery
opposed him in rebellion: thirdly, at the banquet a sudden
gust of wind carried away the crown from his head;

for conveying his body to London. Mr. Wylie (*Henry the Fourth*, i.
114) is inclined to fix the date of Richard's death as early as the
middle of January.

An interesting fact in connection with the above-mentioned minute
of the Privy Council has hitherto escaped observation. When examining the original rough minutes of the council preserved in the
Cottonian library (Cleopatra F. iij. f. 9), I was struck with the care
with which an alteration in this particular minute had been made,
and then discovered that the minute as we now have it is not the
one which was first written. This has been destroyed. The first leaf
of the proceedings of this session of the council contains on its face
nine memoranda or heads of business to be discussed, with this title:
" Fait a remembrer de certains matires necessairs a monsterer au
grant conseil du Roy." The first memorandum is: " En primes si R.
nadgairs Roy soit uncore vivant a ce que len suppose quil est, ordenez
soit quil soit bien et seurement gardez pur sauvacion de lestat du
Roi et de son Roiaume." On the back of the leaf are written four
rough minutes in answer to the first four memoranda. The minute
(the one with which we are concerned) which answers to the first
memorandum runs thus: " A le primer article soit parle au Roi qen
cas qe R. soit vivant, quil soit mys en seuretee g. [aggreable a] les
seignurs et qe sil soit mort qadonqes il soit monstrez overtement au
poeple quils en puissent avoir conissance." Now the leaf is composed
of three pieces of vellum which are connected together so as to form
one sheet. The first piece of vellum, which is a very narrow strip,
contains the first memorandum only; the second piece, the second,
third, and fourth memoranda; and the third piece, the rest. The
minutes in answer to the second, third, and fourth memoranda are
written immediately at their back; but the first minute, instead of
being written directly behind its memorandum, and on the first piece
of vellum, as one would expect, is entered below the fourth minute
and on the third piece of vellum. The reason of this is apparent
after examining the different pieces of vellum, for it is clear that
the second piece has been cut away at the top, part of the words
of the second minute having been docked in the process, and that
the first narrow piece is an addition to take the place of what has
been cut away. There can be no doubt that what took place was
as follows:—The first four memoranda were all written on one piece
(now represented, in a curtailed form, by the second piece) of vellum,
and the four minutes were written on the back in proper order. The

whence, in the third and last place, he was set aside from his kingdom and supplanted by king Henry [1].

And now, Richard, fare thee well !, king indeed (if I may call thee so) most mighty ; for after death all might praise thee, hadst thou, with the help of God and thy people, so ordered thy deeds as to deserve such praise.   But, though well endowed as Solomon, though fair as Absalom, though glorious as Ahasuerus, though a builder excellent as the great Belus, yet, like Chosroes, king of Persia, who was

first minute was, however, reconsidered, and was re-written below. But, as the matter to which it related was one of so serious a nature, it was thought proper to destroy the original draft.  The clerk therefore cut it away, and necessarily, along with it, the first memorandum on the other side.  He then re-wrote the latter on the narrow strip which he fastened to the head of the sheet, as we now have it.  On the back of this narrow strip is the heading: "L'informacion de certains matires a monstrer a grant conseil nostre seignur le Roy," which, however, has no connection with the minutes, but which happened to be on the sheet which the clerk used for the fresh transcript.  As a further proof how anxiously must have been considered the form in which the minute was to appear, the words : "seuretee g. les seignurs," which are an alteration, are written over an erasure very carefully made ; whereas, in the second minute, which contains no state secret, but which has been much altered, most of the corrected words are only crossed out with the pen.  Sir Harris Nicolas has made use of the contemporary fair copy of the minutes in the text of his work (*Proceedings of the Privy Council*, 1834, i. 111), and has inserted the rough minutes in a foot-note ; but, by a strange oversight, not noticing that the first rough minute was written below the others, he has omitted it altogether.

[1] A parallel is to be found in a chronicle which exists in two MSS. in the British Museum : Cotton, Titus D. xv., and Royal 13 A. xix. :— "Hoc eciam anno Ricardus rex in castello de Pounfreit existens, postquam audivit certum nuncium de morte comitum Huntyngdonie, Sarum, et Kancie, et maxime comitis Huntyngdonie, fratris sui, scilicet Johannis Holland, juravit se cibum nunquam pre dolore commesturum ; et sic per quinque dies totidemque noctes a cibariis custoditus circa festum Purificacionis Beate Marie obiit, ut adimpleretur prophecia cujusdam militis Francie ad ejus coronacionem existentis, ubi vidit regis sotularem ad terram cadentem et regem ad prandium cibum suum evomentem.  Quod sic exposuit: 'Iste rex gloriosus erit et in cibis valde habundans, sed regni dignitatem amittet, et in fine pre fame morietur.' "

delivered into the hands of Heraclius, didst thou in the A.D. 1400. midst of thy glory, as Fortune turned her wheel, fall most miserably into the hands of duke Henry, amid the smothered curses of thy people.

Meanwhile the lord Despencer, lord of Glamorgan, as knowing and abetting the treason, was most foully beheaded by workmen at Bristol [1]; and the heads of those who thus fell were fixed on stakes and were for some time shown to the people beyond London-bridge. But, seeing that all these things were done only by the savage fury of the people, I fear that they will make this a plea to wield still more in future against their lords the possession of the sword, which hath now been allowed to them against all system of order.

Also, all blank charters, in which throughout England his subjects had placed themselves under their seals at the will of king Richard, as though there had been a new conquest of the realm, were publicly carried to London on the points of spears, and there burned along with their countless seals.

The bishop of Norwich, uncle of the said lord Despencer, being accused of the same treason, was not delivered to a temporal prison, but to the keeping of my lord of Canterbury, from reverence for his priestly office, to await judgement. But afterwards the king frankly restored him to his church and dignity [2].

---

[1] Thomas Despencer, baron Despencer, was created earl of Gloucester in 1397, but was degraded from that dignity by parliament in 1399. His ancestor, Hugh Despencer, the younger, became possessed of nearly the whole of the county of Glamorgan by his marriage with Eleanor de Clare, the niece of Edward II. He took part in the conspiracy, but escaped from Cirencester when Kent and Salisbury were killed. He was, however, immediately captured and carried to Bristol, and was there beheaded by the mob, on the 15th January.

[2] Henry, bishop of Norwich, was a younger brother of Edward, baron Despencer, the father of Thomas, baron Despencer, who was killed at Bristol. His arrest for complicity in the plot does not appear to be noticed elsewhere.

A.D. 1400.    The bishop of Carlisle, late a monk of Westminster, being
accused of the said treason before the king's justices, was
convicted and condemned by a jury of laymen, and after
languishing for a season in chains in prison in the Tower of
London, his bishopric being given to another, he was sent
back to his old monastery to lead a monk's life, though
named to the see of Miletus (?)[1].

In this year my lord of Canterbury, calling together his
clergy, mournfully laid before them how temporal powers
fear not to violate the liberties of the church of England,
and specially in seizing, imprisoning, and in judging bishops,
without distinction, just as they would laymen. "True!
my lord," I said, " in turning over the corpus of the law
and the chronicles more cruelty is found to have been
inflicted on prelates in England than in all Christendom."
And I quoted the chapter : " Sicut dignum,"[2] touching
homicide, and many others, and in short, as to the present
case of imprisoning bishops, the Clementine chapter : " Si
quis suadente,"[3] touching penalties, which was decreed on
account of the imprisonment of the bishop of Lichfield[4], in
the time of Edward the second, king of England. My lord
of Canterbury then recounted how that but lately Simon

---

[1] Thomas Merke, or Merks, the favourite of Richard II., who
remained true to his master to the last, and who is best known by the
famous speech which Shakespeare puts into his mouth on slender
authority. He was brought to trial at the end of January, and, after
being found guilty, he was deprived of his bishopric. He was removed
from the Tower to the custody of the abbot of Westminster on the
23rd June. On the 28th November he was pardoned, and was afterwards treated by Henry with lenience and generosity. The pope had
translated him to a titular see, "ad ecclesiam de Samastone." This
see has been variously identified with Samos, Samos in Cephalonia,
and Samothrace. But it has been more recently suggested that it was
Samosata; and that the "Millatencis pontificatus" of Adam of Usk is
a see (be it that of Miletus or what it may) to which there is some
reason to believe that Merke was translated in 1402 (*Dict. Nat. Biog.*
xxxvij. 284). He died rector of Todenham in Gloucestershire, in 1409.

[2] Decret. Greg. IX., lib. v., tit. xij. §. vj.

[3] Decret. Clement. lib. v., tit. viij. §. i.      [4] Walter de Langton.

Islip, his predecessor, seeing his suffragan, Thomas Lylde, then bishop of Ely, dragged as a criminal in Westminster hall and standing before the judgement-seat of the king's justices, did take him by the right hand saying: "Thou art my subject. Thou art standing in forbidden court before him who is not thy judge. Come with me." And so, in spite of the judge, he led him away. Yet the bishop, not daring to remain in England, gat him to the court of Rome; and there he caused that judge to be excommunicated, and, for that he had in the meantime died, to be bereft of church burial and cast out into a ditch[1].

Having heard that France and Scotland were making them ready to invade England, the king, taxing only the lords spiritual and temporal, did spare the commons[2].

The body of lord Richard, late king of England, was brought to the church of Saint Paul in London, the face not covered but shown openly to all; and the rites being there celebrated on that night and a mass on the morrow, he was buried at Langley among the Dominican friars. My God!, how many thousand marks he spent on burial-places of vainglory, for himself and his wives, among the kings at Westminster! But Fortune ordered it otherwise.

Brother William Botsam died, bishop of Rochester, sometime of Llandaff, and master John Botsam, chancellor of my lord of Canterbury, was raised to his place[3]. There died also that man of grace, John ap Griffith, abbot of

---

[1] Thomas Lylde (not William Lyle, as in the MS.), bishop of Ely, was put on his trial and condemned for the homicide, by one of his servants, of a follower of the lady Blanche de Wake. Godwin (*De præsulibus Angliæ*) seems to imply that Simon Drayton, one of the judges, was refused burial in accordance with the terms of excommunication.

[2] The lords agreed to furnish ships and men, and to maintain them for three months; the clergy were to contribute a tenth in lieu of personal service.—Wylie, *Henry the Fourth*, i. 125.

[3] William de Bottlesham, translated from Llandaff to Rochester in 1389, died in February, 1400. John de Bottlesham, his successor, died in 1404.

A.D. 1400. Llanthony, who, when his monastery was by accident
burned to the ground, in a few years marvellously restored
it from its foundations. To him succeeded a man of the
highest prudence, John ap Hoel, prior of the same house.

In this Lent, the lads[1] of the city of London, often
gathering together in thousands and choosing kings among
themselves, made war upon each other, and fought to their
utmost strength; whereby many died stricken with blows,
or trampled under foot, or crushed in narrow ways—much
to the wonder of the people what this might foreshow:
which I believe was the plague that happened next year,
wherein the greater number of them departed this life. Yet
from such gatherings could they not be restrained, until
the king wrote to their parents and masters with grievous
threats to prevent them.

On the third day of the month of May, the prince bestowed upon me a prebend in the church of Bangor.

Also, on the fourth day of the same month of May, our
lord the king being seated in judgement in his hall within
the Tower of London in right royal state, my lord Morley,
who had lately appealed the earl of Salisbury of treason[2],
for that the said earl, on the day appointed for the combat,
answered not to the third summons, prayed that he be
adjudged traitor according to the form of the appeal, and
that his pledges be condemned in costs. And I, although
a chaplain, by sentence and judgement made suit in his
name, because the earl, as is aforesaid, was dead. The
other side made exception on his death, that it took place
before the appointed day. Whereupon I rejoined that by
treasonable rebellion he caused his own death, and so he
fell by his own assault, quoting the law: "Si decesserit,"
in the title: "Qui satisdare cogantur"[3] in the Digest;

---

[1] i.e. apprentices.

[2] Thomas de Morley, fourth baron Morley. The trial by battle
was to have taken place at Newcastle-on-Tyne.

[3] Digest, ii. tit. viij. l. 4.

and again: "Si homo sisti," law: "Si eum"[1]; title: A.D. 1400.
"Si quis cautionibus"[2]; and title: "Judicatum solvi,"
law: "Judicatum"[3]; and the codex: "De custodia reo-
rum," law: "Ad Commentariensem.[4]" And in short my
side had colour against the pledges of the said earl, and
paid me a fee of one hundred shillings and twelve yards of
scarlet cloth.

In this year, that is, in the year of our Lord 1400, a great
plague prevailed through all England, and specially among
the young, swift in its attack and carrying off many souls.
Then died my lord John of Usk, abbot of Chertsey, together
with thirteen monks. He, of happy memory, an inceptor
in theology, a man surely of the greatest holiness, ever
walking as a servant of the Blessed Virgin, gave up his
soul to the Lord on the day of her Nativity (8th September)
—just as he had ever wished it to happen on that feast,
being born in her parish and baptized at her font in Usk.
Would I might be worthy to go with him on his way!
I was with him in his last moments, and I had his blessing,
wherein I rejoice, in these words: "The blessing which the
Blessed Virgin gave to her son, our Lord Jesus; the blessing
which Isaac gave to his son Jacob, I give to thee." Being
comforted in his sleep by the Blessed Virgin, as he was
departing he spake thus to his brethren and to me: "The
enemy laid snares for me, but the Blessed Virgin Mary,
coming with other two ladies to my succour, did utterly
drive him out, giving me comfort that henceforth he should
not trouble me, and that she herself with those two would
not leave me, until she had my soul safe with her." And
then as it were a gentle sleep fell upon him. And a certain
brother, William Burton, roused him, saying: "Be of good
cheer, for you shall fare well!" The abbot replied: "Blessed
be God! I shall fare well. Be silent and hearken!" The
monk said: "Unto what shall I hearken?" "The host of

---

[1] Digest, ii. tit. ix. l. 10.     [2] Ibid. tit. xj.
[3] Ibid. xlvi. tit. vij. l. 6.    [4] Codex, ix. tit. iv. l. 4.

angels singing with sweetest melody, ' Come, blessed son of thy heavenly Father, receive his kingdom for thine eternal inheritance.'" The other said: " I hear it not. Would I were worthy to hear!" And so he peacefully rendered his soul to God.

In the same year the king passed into Scotland with a great and glorious host to tame the fierceness of the Scots [1]. But they, fleeing to places of refuge, laid waste and stripped their fields and houses and farms, lest they should profit our king; and, lurking in thickets and in the hiding-places of secret caves and woods, they withdrew before the king's face. Yet did they often issue forth from these lairs, and in lonely deserts and by-paths they slew and took prisoners very many of our men, doing us more harm than we did to them.

On the day of the Decollation of Saint John the Baptist (29th August) the king returned into England; and hearing at Leicester how Owen, lord of Glendower, along with the Northern Welsh who had raised him up to be their prince, had broken out into rebellion and had seized many castles, and how he had burned on all sides the towns wherein the English dwelt amongst them, pillaging them and driving out the English, he gathered together the flower of his troops, and marched his array into North Wales. And the Welsh being subdued and driven away, their prince with seven others lay hid for a year among rocks and caves. With others who yielded peacefully the king dealt gently, slaying but very few of them, yet carrying away their chieftains captive to Shrewsbury. But afterwards he set them free, on condition of pursuing and taking those who still held out in rebellion in Snowdon and elsewhere.

About the feast of Saint Faith (6th October) [2], the earl

---

[1] Henry crossed the border on the 14th August.

[2] The only important success of the English after Henry's retirement was that won, on the 29th September, by sir Richard Umfraville, at Redeswere, over a large Scottish force (Wylie, *Henry the Fourth*,

of Northumberland and his son, the lord Henry Percy, had
a great battle with the Scots who were invading England
after the king's withdrawal : wherein they took one hundred knights and squires of the Scots and put the rest to
flight.  The victory was won thus : the English grooms in
the rear, mounting their masters' horses during the battle,
did very craftily and with success use a stratagem of war,
shouting with one voice : " The Scots flee ! The Scots
flee !," whereat the Scots who fought in the forefront of
the battle were too sorely scared ; and, while they looked
behind them to find out the truth thereof, they fell stricken
down by a storm of blows from maces about their ears and
shoulders.

On the king's behalf this writ was issued to me, the
writer of this history : "The king to his beloved master
Adam of Usk, doctor of laws, greeting.  We send unto you,
in writing, under our seal, certain matters of doubt which
concern the estate and honour of our realm, carefully re-
quiring and strictly commanding you that, after examining
into the same with good and mature deliberation and fully
understanding the matter, you do send in writing your
prudent advice and answer, wherein you shall by law
maintain your points in each particular, to us or to our
council, before the feast of Saint Michael next ensuing,
laying aside all excuse and raising no difficulty.  And
furthermore, on account of the diverse opinions of others
skilled in the law, which perchance might delay the
advancement of that business, we will and command that
you be in your own person before our said council, at
Westminster, on the octave of the same feast, together with
those who shall be joined with you as counsel in that
deliberation, there, all of you, to set forth your advice in
those matters, and to bring those opinions to one end and
conclusion.  And this by the troth whereby you are

i. 140).  It seems as if Adam had confounded some such action with
the Percys' victory at Homildon Hill in 1402.

A.D. 1400. bounden unto us, and as you love the honour and safety of the estate of our realm, you shall in no wise neglect. Witness myself at Westminster, on the twelfth day of September, in the first year of our reign." [1]

"Follow questions on articles touching the marriage entered into between the lord Richard, late king of England, and the lady Isabella, daughter of the king of France. And first, the motives and causes leading to the contract of such marriage do follow :—

"In the treaty late had by reason of the marriage between Richard, king of England, and the daughter of the king of France,—a hope being raised that the countless great and common offences, evils, inconveniences, wrongs, and shedding of human blood, which by reason of the strifes and wars between the two kingdoms, etc., have hitherto come to pass, might henceforth cease; and that, in better wise and more quickly, good conclusions, peace and concord might be had between the said kingdoms, long to last in times to come ; and that the bond of relationship might exist between those kings and their successors ; besides, that friendship and intercourse might be wonderfully fostered between their realms and subjects—among other things, it was agreed that the said queen be joined in marriage with the said Richard, and that the king of France, in regard of that marriage, do pay to the said king Richard eight hundred thousand francs; whereof five hundred thousand francs have been paid.

"It was also agreed that, if after solemnization of the said marriage the king of England should decease without children begotten of the said marriage, and if the said

---

[1] A letter, under date of 12th Nov. 1400, was sent to Oxford, submitting questions on this matter. It is printed in Rymer's *Fœdera*, but the questions do not appear. Isabella's dower amounted to 800,000 francs, of which 300,000 were payable on the marriage, and the remaining 500,000 in five yearly instalments. This last sum was repayable if Richard died without children by the marriage.

queen should survive the king, she being under age or not
of the age of twelve years fully completed, then the sum of
five hundred thousand francs, or whatever should have
been paid of the said greater sum over and above the sum
of three hundred thousand francs, be given back to the
said queen: whereunto the said king of England did bind
himself and his heirs and successors and those who should
act for him, and all his goods, moveable and immoveable,
then being and to come; yet did not the consent of the
parliament, that then was, herein intervene.

"Is the king of England, that now is, herein bound by
the lord king Richard and held to the restoration of the
money so received over and above the three hundred
thousand francs, seeing that, in the aforesaid obligation
entered into, as above, by king Richard, the realm had not
given consent? And, if not, will the causes and suggestions
set forth in the treaty of marriage, and related above,
which seem to have regard to the public weal of both
kingdoms, be of force to compell and bind the king, that
now is, to the restoration of such money?

"Also, by virtue of the treaty, our lord the king, that now
is, at the time when he was earl of Derby, and other lords
more near to the royal blood did one and all, for themselves,
their direct heirs, successors, and executors, by their letters
promise, of their certain knowledge and full will, that, if
the said king Richard should decease before the consumma-
tion of the said marriage, the said queen should be restored,
free and released from all bonds and hindrances of the
marriage and from all other obligations whatsoever, along
with all her jewels and goods, to the king of France, her
father, or to his heir and successor; the said earl and
others, the aforesaid lords, binding and straitly pledging
themselves, their heirs, successors, and executors aforesaid,
and all their goods whatsoever, moveable and immoveable,
then being or to come, on behalf of all and every the aforesaid things to be held, observed, done, and wholly fulfilled,

according to the form and tenour of the said letters obligatory and of the treaty of and upon the marriage aforesaid.

"It is asked, how far it is to be understood of such goods: whether only of those which had been delivered with the queen, or as well those as others which had from that time until now been gotten by her; and whether the two hundred thousand francs, whereof mention is above made in the aforesaid treaty of marriage, are to be included under and in such goods?"

"Follow questions on other articles touching three millions of crowns to be paid by the king of France to the king of England:—

"Formerly, in the treaty of final peace between John, king of France, and Edward, king of England, among other things, it was agreed that the king of France should pay to the king of England, or to his deputy, three millions of crowns of gold, at certain stated terms; to which payment the king of France, at Calais, whilst he was in the power of the king of England, did bind himself and his heirs, and their goods moveable and immoveable. Whereof the moiety remains to be paid.

"Can the king of England, that now is, justly claim of the king of France, that now is, such money not yet paid? And, if not, doth action belong to the executors of king Edward? And, if so, can the king of England, that now is, the direct and equitable right being yielded to him by the executors of king Edward, claim the money as assignee?"

"Follows the gist of the letters of the said king of France upon the aforesaid article, wherein are contained the causes of such treaty: 'John, by the grace of God king of France, to one and all now being and to come. We make known unto you by these presents that upon all disagreements and variances whatsoever moved between us, for ourselves and all those whom it may concern of the one part, and the king of England and all those whom it may concern of the other part, for the good of peace, it doth stand agreed, on such a day and in such a place, in manner following: Firstly, that the king of England shall have such castles and such places, etc. Also it is agreed that the king of France shall pay unto the king of England, or to his deputy, three millions of crowns of gold at certain terms,' etc.

" Also, seeing that the king of France, being taken captive in the wars by the king of England, in the agreement of final peace did bind himself and his heirs to pay to the king of England three millions of crowns, whilst the same king of France was at Calais in the power of the king of England, no mention being made in the letters of the said agreement that such payment should be made by reason of discharge of the ransom of the said king of France, is that obligation made void in that it is pretended that fear had influence, notwithstanding that it is well known to all the world that the sum of money was owing for such ransom or discharge ?

" After the said obligation, the aforesaid king of France being at Boulogne and at liberty, as he declared, did in his letters recite that article, wherein it is provided that the king of France should pay to the king of England, or to his deputy, the said sum at the terms agreed on, as aforesaid ; and afterwards in the same letters he makes known that he had paid to his very dear brother, the king of England, a certain sum of money in part-payment of the said larger sum ; and in those letters he bound himself and his heirs, and all their goods whatsoever, to pay to his said brother the remainder not yet paid, willing that all other bonds before made in this behalf be altogether accounted for naught.

" It is asked as before in the said article, and especially whether this second bond of the king of France, made at Boulogne, concerning the aforesaid sum payable to the king of England, doth seem to do away with the first bond made to the king of England or in any way to alter the same, seeing that there appeareth in writing naught distinctly concerning the consent of the same king thereto.

" Also, in another article in the same treaty it is distinctly contained that, the king of France restoring certain strongholds, etc., in like manner the king of England is bound to restore certain other strongholds now held by him and his men.

" If it appear that the king of France hath made surrender of the strongholds, etc., and hath fulfilled all the aforesaid on his behalf, but that the king of England hath not performed his promises, can the payment of the money promised by the king of France to the king of England, as it is contained in the treaty, be justly refused ?

" Also, in another article in the treaty whereof mention is made above, it is contained that the king of France did promise to deliver certain strongholds to the king of England, and likewise, after such delivery, that he should make certain abjurations upon certain rights and jurisdiction and other things ; moreover, that he should make to be delivered in fact and handed over, at a certain time, at Bruges, to the king of England or his deputies, letters touching such abjuration and surrender, sealed with his seal.   And the king of England in like manner promised to surrender certain strongholds, and to renounce his right touching the crown of France, etc.

" If it appear that the king of France, on his side, at the aforesaid day and place, was ready to fulfill all the aforesaid, and if it appear that the king of England performed not the promises made by him in this behalf, nor sent his messengers to Bruges, within the stated time, to receive the promises and offerings of the king of France and to fulfill the promises of the king of England,—can the payment of the money, as aforesaid, promised by the king of France to the king of England, be, on account of the negligence or default of the said king of England, justly refused ?

" Also, if the aforesaid sum not yet paid out of the aforesaid three millions of crowns be owing to our lord the king
of England, by his own right or by the right ceded by the
executors of king Edward, etc., and if it hath so happened
that the same lord the king is held to restore to our lady
the queen, daughter of the king of France, the two hundred
thousand francs, whereof mention is made above,—of such
sums, claimed and owed on this side and that, ought, in
law, a balance thereof to be struck, although the said queen
in this event be deemed a third party, to whom restoration
or payment must be made ? Because, although the restoration of the two hundred thousand francs be made to the
queen herself, yet was the bond in the first place agreed
on and settled between Richard, king of England, and
Charles, now king of France. And thus it appeareth that
the king of England, that now is, in his own right or in
that which is ceded to him, can strike a balance between
the same parties.

" Also, supposing, without prejudice to fact, that the king
of England, that now is, be held, as earl of Derby, to restore
the aforesaid two hundred thousand francs, or can balance
them, as abovesaid, are the other lords, who were bound
along with him as joint-bails or fellow-sureties, held,
according to the terms of their letter, etc., to contribute
toward the payment of those two hundred thousand francs,
or ought the same king first to discount the same two
hundred thousand francs from the goods and jewels of
king Richard ?

" Also, supposing again, without prejudice to fact, that
the king, that now is, is held to give up the queen with
her goods and jewels without let, according to the tenour
of the clause set forth in the treaty,—can the same king,
that now is, making exception in his own right as king of
England, or in the right ceded to him by the executors of
king Edward, as aforesaid, hinder the surrender of the
aforesaid queen with her goods, etc., and make use of his

right of arrest, until the king of France shall be willing to make satisfaction to the king, that now is, of the remainder of the three million crowns, which, as is well known, is still due and unpaid?

"To put the question shortly :—Can the king of England, that now is, put forward the aforesaid exception of the unpaid remainder, or any other exception, which shall have force to hinder the surrender of the queen with her goods, until the king of France shall be able to break down or remove such exception?

" Also, the ambassadors of our lord the king, that now is, at Calais, finally promised in the treaty to the ambassadors of the king of France to give up the queen with her goods without let before the feast of the Purification of Our Lady next following, according to the tenour of the bond thereon made.

"If the council of the king of France, or of the same queen, shall refuse first of all to give an acquittance in fact on such surrender, which might sweep away and altogether root out evils without end and cause of offence and human bloodshed (and yet it is likely that all these will otherwise come about by reason of this marriage, as hath often happened between England and France, in times gone by, in like conjunctures), can the aforesaid ambassadors thereupon refuse to give up the queen together with her goods, notwithstanding promise made, and saving too the honour of king and kingdom, until the others shall be willing to deliver such exclusory acquittance, etc.?

" Also, formerly in the treaty of final peace, whereof in the third point above, it was among other things agreed between the same kings, as is declared, although it appeareth not in writing, that king Edward should cause to be driven out and wholly withdrawn, within a fixed time, at his own cost, all his mercenaries and others his subjects who were overrunning the realm of France.

"If it appear that king Edward fulfilled not his promises

within the said term, but did afford in arms help, counsel, A.D. 1400. and favour to the same his mercenaries and other subjects, it being clear as to the said agreement in the first treaty of peace or after that treaty,—can payment of the said remainder of the three million crowns be justly refused on that score?"

On the twenty-fifth day of September, the most noble lady, my lady Philippa, daughter of my lord the earl of March, who was wedded first to that most proper youth the earl of Pembroke who was slain in a tourney at Woodstock, and next to the noble earl of Arundel who was beheaded, and thirdly to the lord Saint John, a little while after she had presented me to the church of West Hanningfield in Essex, and before she had yet reached her four-and-twentieth year, went the way of all flesh at Halnaker by Chichester, and lies buried in the priory of Boxgrove [1].

The Lombards and other merchants from beyond seas in London, who had been wont to dwell in their own inns and had been allowed freely to offer their merchandise for sale, were now, after the foreign fashion, so restrained, that they might not dwell by themselves, but in the house of some citizen who should stand surety; nor were they allowed in any way to offer their goods for sale, except under the care of the same citizen.

The duke of Bavaria, brother of the queen of France, was, by the aid of the French, raised up to be emperor, the king of Bohemia, who for long while had held the empire, being despised as useless and as not yet having been crowned by the pope; but he was defeated in a stricken field together with many of the French by the same king [2].

[1] Philippa, daughter of Edmund, third earl of March, married first John Hastings, third earl of Pembroke, killed 30th December, 1391, *æt.* 17; secondly, Richard Fitzalan, fourth earl of Arundel; and thirdly, Thomas Poynings, baron Saint John.

[2] Wenceslaus, or Wenzel, king of Bohemia, who became emperor in 1378, was deposed by a majority of the electors in 1400; and

Four little bells, hanging at the four corners of the shrine of Saint Edward at Westminster, ringing of their own accord and with more than human power, miraculously sounded four times in one day, to the great awe and wonder of the brethren.

The spring wherein the head of Llewellyn ap Griffith, last prince of Wales, was washed after that it was cut off, and which is in the village of Builth, throughout a livelong day did flow in an unmixed stream of blood [1].

One thing in these days I grieve to tell, to wit, that two popes, like to a monster in nature, now for two and twenty years [2], most wickedly rending the seamless coat of Christ, contrary to the words of the Song of Solomon: "My dove is but one," [3] have too sorely vexed the world by leading astray men's souls, and racking their bodies with divers terrors.   And woeful it is, if it be true what I call to mind in the text of Scripture: "Ye are the salt of the earth; but if the salt have lost his savour, wherewith shall it be salted? It is thenceforth good for nothing, but to be cast out, and to be trodden under foot of men." [4]   Whence, seeing that the priesthood was become venal, did not Christ, making him a scourge of small cords, drive out them that bought and sold in the temple?   And hence I fear lest we, with many stripes and spurnings, be cast out from the glory of the priesthood.   For I take heed that in the Old

Rupert III., a duke of Bavaria and count-palatine of the Rhine, was chosen in his place. The new emperor succeeded in overcoming opposition, and was crowned on the 6th January, 1401. Adam is wrong in calling him the brother of the queen of France. Isabella of Bavaria, queen of Charles VI., was of another family, being the daughter of Stephen, duke of Bavaria-Ingolstadt.

[1] Llewellyn was defeated and slain by John Gifford and sir Edmund Mortimer, in 1282. His head, with a silver crown on it, was set up in Cheapside, in derision of the prophecy that he was to wield the sceptre of Brutus and ride through Cheapside with a crown on his head.—Thomas, *Memoirs of Owen Glendower* (1822), p. 13.

[2] The papal schism began in 1378, by the elections of Urban VI and Clement VII.          [3] Ch. vj. 9.          [4] Matt. v. 13.

Testament, after that venality had corrupted the priest- A.D. 1400. hood, the cloud of smoke, the unquenchable fire, and the sweet smell which hurteth not ceased in the temple. In short, lo! the virgin mother, according to the word of Revelation [1], hath fled with the man child into the wilderness from the face of the beast that sitteth upon the throne. But here Plato bids me hold my peace; for there is nothing more certain than death, nothing more uncertain than the hour of death. And so, blessed be God! I, already making my preparation for death, leave in my native church, that is, of Usk, my memorial in a suitable missal, and a grail, and a tropar, and a sequence-book, and an antiphonal, newly written and drawn up with new additions and notes, and in a full suit of vestments, with three copes, broidered with my bearings, that is: on a field sable, a naked man delving; and I commend myself to the suffrages of prayers offered up therein. Further, I have in view, if God grant it, to adorn the same church with more worthy repair, to the glory of the Blessed Virgin, in honour of whose Nativity it is dedicated; yet do I not reckon this to mine own praise, for God forbid that this record of my foolishness should be seen in my lifetime!

The eldest son of France was made duke of Aquitaine, in disinheritance and in defiance of the king of England; and, he dying, the second son, taking his place, passed with an army into the parts of Aquitaine to subdue it [2].

The emperor of the Greeks [3], seeking to get aid against the Saracens, visited the king of England in London, on

---

[1] xij. 14.

[2] Louis, duke of Guienne and dauphin of France, at this time only six years old, did not die till 1415, when he was succeeded by his brother John, who, in his turn, died in 1417, and gave place to Charles, afterwards king.

[3] Manuel II. Palæologus. He travelled into western Europe at this time, in order to solicit help against the Turks who were besieging Constantinople. He landed in England on the 11th December. See Wylie, *Henry the Fourth*, ch. ix.

the day of Saint Thomas the Apostle (21st December), being well received by him, and abiding with him, at very great cost, for two months, being also comforted at his departure with very great gifts. This emperor always walked with his men, dressed alike and in one colour, namely white, in long robes cut like tabards; he finding fault with the many fashions and distinctions in dress of the English[1], wherein he said that fickleness and changeable temper was betokened. No razor touched head or beard of his chaplains. These Greeks were most devout in their church services, which were joined in as well by soldiers as by priests, for they chanted them without distinction in their native tongue. I thought within myself, what a grievous thing it was that this great Christian prince from the farther east should perforce be driven by unbelievers to visit the distant islands of the west, to seek aid against them. My God! What dost thou, ancient glory of Rome? Shorn is the greatness of thine empire this day; and truly may the words of Jeremy be spoken unto thee: "Princess among the provinces, how is she become tributary!"[2] Who would ever believe that thou shouldst sink to such depth of misery, that, although once seated on the throne of majesty thou didst lord it over all the world, now thou hast no power to bring succour to the Christian faith?

The king kept Christmas with the emperor at Eltham.

My lord of Canterbury sent the abbot of Leicester and me to the nuns' priory of Nuneaton, in the diocese of Lichfield, to make inquest against sir Robert Bowland, touching divers crimes, heresies, and errors there, as was

---

[1] These were the "duche cotis," as Langland (*Richard the Redeles*) calls the German-cut clothes said to have been imported with Anne of Bohemia, conspicuous with

"A wondir curiose crafte y-come now of late,

That men clepith kerving þe cloþe all to pecis,"

and with "sleves þat slode uppon þe erthe."

[2] Lament. i. 1.

evilly spread abroad, by him, like a serpent under the disguise of pretended holiness, wickedly committed. And then and there we found that a certain nun, by the unbounded lust of the same Robert, had become pregnant in an unnatural way, as appeared as well by the confession of the same nun as by the letters of the said Robert, and also by a view of her body taken by matrons before the birth; and that she had thereby, on the feast of Saint Petronilla (31st May) last past, borne a daughter who was like to the said Robert. And this did Robert himself confess in full convocation of the clergy.

On the octave of Saint Hilary (20th January), the king held a solemn parliament in London, at Westminster. And my lord of Canterbury held a great convocation of the clergy in St. Paul's church [1].

In the time of this parliament, the lord Grey of Ruthin, heir by intestacy of the earl of Pembroke and lord of Hastings, being admitted in the court of chivalry of England, moved a costly suit against the lord Edward Hastings, touching the arms of Hastings, to wit: a manche or, on a field gules, which the latter bore as his rightfully, claiming thus to be heir in this behalf. And herein he retained me of his counsel. In this suit, the lord William Beauchamp, lord of Bergavenny, for that he, by gift of the said earl if he should die without heirs of his body begotten, with the king's leave, had a moiety of that lordship and of others which belonged to the earl, for his own advantage worked manfully with the said lord Grey; and no wonder, for the victory of the said Edward would cause both to be utterly barred [2].

---

[1] The members of parliament assembled on the 20th, but the session actually commenced on the 21st January. Convocation met on the 29th of the month.

[2] Reginald, baron Grey of Ruthin, grandson of Roger, baron Grey of Ruthin, by Elizabeth, daughter of John, baron Hastings (*ob.* 1313), was adjudged heir of John Hastings, third earl of Pembroke (*ob.* 1391), great-great-grandson of the same baron Hastings. Edward, baron

A.D. 1401. In convocation, a certain sir William Sawtre, chaplain, being found guilty of, and condemned for, heresy, straight-way, on such sentence being delivered against him, with great heat spake to my lord of Canterbury these words: "I, sent by God, declare to thee that thou and all thy clergy and the king also shall die anon an evil death; and the tongue of a strange people shall hold sway in the land. And this evil standeth waiting even in the gates." And he being thus condemned, having first been solemnly degraded, was afterwards, in Smithfield, in London, chained standing to a post in a barrel, packed round with blazing faggots, and was thus burned to ashes [1].

In the time of this parliament, at Lent, one William Clerk, a writer of Canterbury, but born in the county of Chester, was condemned by judgement of the court mili-tary, and was first reft of his tongue, for that he had uttered against the king wicked words, laying them to the charge of others, and then of his right hand where-with he had written them, and lastly by penalty of talion, because he made not good his charges, was beheaded at the Tower.

Ambassadors of state, on behalf of the duke of Bavaria, who had been, as above said, lately elected to the empire,

Hastings, was son of Hugh, baron Hastings, of Gressing Hall, co. Norf., great-grandson of the half-blood of the same John, baron Hastings. William Beauchamp, baron Bergavenny, was son of Thomas Beau-champ, earl of Warwick, by Katherine, daughter of Roger Mortimer, earl of March, and sister of Agnes, wife of Lawrence Hastings, first earl of Pembroke and lord of Bergavenny. The suit for the arms was decided in favour of lord Grey, after lasting twenty years.

[1] William Chatrys, or Sawtery, or Sawtre, formerly chaplain or parish priest of St. Margaret's, King's Lynn, and of Tilney, co. Norfolk. He was charged with heresy before Henry Spencer, bishop of Norwich, and was condemned; but he recanted and was pardoned, 6th February, 1400. He then became chaplain of St. Osyth in Walbrook, and, again preaching heresy, he was brought before con-vocation, 12th February, 1401. He was convicted, publicly degraded in St. Paul's on the 26th February, and burned on the 2nd March.

arrived in England, for the marriage of the king's daughter
with him [1].  And I said to them aside: "Is not the king
of Bohemia elected and in possession of the empire?  Why
then this new election, with the former one not quashed?"
One of them, who was a priest of rank, answered me:
"Because he was useless, and, as he was not yet crowned
by the pope, the electors have thus done in this behalf."
Then said I: "By the chapter: 'Venerabilem,' in the title:
'De electionibus,' [2] it is acknowledged that this power
belongeth to the pope alone, because he himself did carry
over the empire from the Greeks to the Germans."  Then
the bishop of Hereford bade me hold my peace.

From this priest I had these two verses against simony,
which did please me:—

"These two evils shalt thou bear, if that thou be Simon's
    heir:
Thou shalt burn when thou art dead; living, thou shalt
    want thy bread."

But now as to what is touched on above concerning the
election of the emperor, and how many and what crowns
he hath, and by whom he is elected and receives them, and
what they mean.  There are seven electors, whence these
verses:—

    "From Maintz and Trier and eke Cologne
    Come chancellors for Cæsar's throne.
    A steward, the palgrave serves his lord;
    And Saxony doth bear the sword.

[1] Negotiations for the marriage of Henry's daughter, Blanche, with
Louis Barbatus, son of Rupert, count-palatine and emperor of Germany, which took place in 1402.  Rupert sent three commissioners
to treat with Henry, on the 9th January.  Two of them were knights;
the third was "Thilmannus de Smalenborch, decanus ecclesiæ Beatæ
Mariæ ad gradus Coloniensis," the priest of rank with whom Adam
conversed (*Fœdera*, viij. 170).  The terms of the contract of marriage
were settled by the 7th March.

[2] Decret. Greg. IX. lib. i. tit. vj. § 34.

As chamberlain a marquis bends;
Bohemia's king the wine-cup tends.
On whom these princes' choice doth fall,
He reigneth over-lord of all."[1]

Extract: "De re judicata"; chapter: "Ad apostolicæ";
penultimate gloss of Johannes Andreæ [2].

The first crown, which is of iron, in token of valour,
shall the archbishop of Cologne give to the elect; the
second, of silver, in token of chastity, shall the archbishop
of Trier give; the third, of gold, in token of excellence,
shall the archbishop of Maintz give, and this last shall the
pope, in the confirmation of the elect, place upon his head
as he kneels at his feet in token of humility and to do
honour to the holy Roman church, whose vassal he is.

It was ordained, in this parliament, that the men of the
marches might use reprisals against Welshmen who were
their debtors or who had injured them, a truce of a week
for making amends being first had [3].

Also, on behalf of the prelates, it was proposed that,
whereas they are summoned to parliament as barons and
so hold their temporalities of the king, therefore their rank
is not lower than that of the other patrons of the kingdom,
as to collation of benefices. But the commons stood out
for papal provision in relief of the universities and the
clergy. The prelates then undertook of their own free

---

[1] Another version of the lines appears in the Antwerp edition of
the Sextus of 1573:

"Magna Maguntia, crassa Colonia, Treveris alma,
Atque Palatinus dapifer, dux portitor ensis,
Marchio præpositus cameræ, pincerna Bohemus,
Romanum regem statuendi dant sibi legem."

[2] Sext. Decret. lib. ii. tit. xiv., "De sententia et re judicata,"
§. ij., "Papa Imperatorem deponere potest ex causis legitimis," beginning with the words "Ad apostolicæ."

[3] See Rot. Parl. iij. 474, for the ordinance sanctioning reprisals
against the Welsh.

will to make provision of benefices within the kingdom A.D. 1401. to pious clerks[1].

I knew a certain monk in the Charter-house, near to London, who was of good health and strong, though he fasted of his own will from all kinds of food for a whole fortnight together. Whereupon the prior of the house, whose counsel I was, put the question to me, whether, if the man should in such case die, he would deserve to enjoy church burial.

In this parliament and convocation there were granted unto the king by the clergy a tenth and a half, and by the people a fifteenth of all goods, with two shillings from every tun of wine, and from other merchandise eight pence in the pound, though with much murmuring and smothered curses of clergy and people.

This parliament was ended on the tenth day of the month of March; about which time, a little before, I heard debated very many harsh things to be put in force against the Welsh, to wit: that they should not marry with the English, nor get them wealth nor dwell in England, and many other grievous things. And, as God knoweth me, the night before, there roused me from my sleep a voice thus sounding in mine ears: "The plowers plowed upon my back," etc., "The Lord is righteous," etc., as in the psalm: "Many a time have they afflicted me."[2] Whence having awoke, and dreading that that day should bring me forth some mishap, I fearfully commended myself to the special governance of the Holy Ghost[3].

---

[1] See *Rot. Parl.* iij. 458, 465, touching relaxation of the statute of provisors. The commons petitioned, on behalf of the universities of Oxford and Cambridge, that the king would hold them in special remembrance, "queux sont founteins de Clergie en ceste Roialme, et par especial les Graduatz, en relevation et sustentation de la Clergie et de la Foie Catholike."

[2] Ps. cxxix.

[3] See the ordinances, 18th March, 1401. *Fœdera*, viij. 184.

*Here followeth the year of our Lord 1401[1].*

The earl of Warwick, a man of most kindly nature, of whom I have spoken above, having been delivered from prison[2], was taken from this life on Good Friday (1st April), a day which he was wont to honour by large alms, penances, and other deeds of devotion in many ways, and changed the fleeting things of earth for those which last for ever in heaven, leaving an only son his heir, to whom the king, giving him grace of two years of nonage, delivered his inheritance.

William ap Tudor and Rhys ap Tudor, brothers, natives of the isle of Anglesey, or Mona, because they could not have the king's pardon for Owen's rebellion[3], on the same Good Friday seized the castle of Conway, which was well stored with arms and victuals, the two warders being slain by the craftiness of a certain carpenter who feigned to come to his accustomed work; and, entering therein with other forty men, they held it for a stronghold. But, straightway being beleaguered by the prince and the country, on the twenty-eighth day of May next following they surrendered the same castle, cowardly for themselves and treacherously for their comrades; for, having bound nine of their number, who were very hateful to the prince, by stealth as they slept after the night watches, they gave them up, on condition of saving their own and the others' lives. And the nine thus bound and yielded up to the prince they straightway saw drawn, disembowelled, hanged, beheaded, and quartered.

[1] Commencing in the Old Style on the 25th March.

[2] He was set at liberty by Henry, and was restored in blood and honours, in 1399. The date of his death is usually stated to be the 8th April.

[3] William ap Tudor and Rhys ap Tudor were excepted, with Owen Glendower, in the pardon granted to the people of Anglesey, Merioneth, etc., 10th March, 1401. They surrendered the castle on condition of pardon.

At this same time certain men of the town of Usk, A.D. 1401. secretly leaving the church during the service of the Passion of our Lord, entered by craft into the castle, and, breaking his prison, set free one John Fitz Pers, late seneschal therein, who, having been accused by evil report of adultery with a certain lady [1], had been, to all men's wonder, condemned to mortal penalty by sir Edward Cherleton, who was only her natural brother, and now lay naked undergoing punishment; and they gave him up, to their great delight, to the lord Bergavenny in his castle. Yet he was afterwards on this account exiled by the king for seduction.

In these days [Tamerlane], the son of the king of Persia, A.D. 1402. conquered and took captive in a stricken field the soldan of the Turks of Babylon, called "Ilderim," [2] who had struck great dread into Christendom, as boasting that he would destroy the faith, and who had been wont to invade the Christians, and especially the Hungarians, with a hundred thousand warriors; and he utterly destroyed Jerusalem, and held those parts with great state. Wherefore the pilgrimage of Christians to those parts is now hindered.

On the first day of May, at Norton St. Philip, the cloth A.D. 1401. merchants slew, in the middle of the market-place, a certain

---

[1] The words "de adulterio cum domina quadam quia diffamatum" are an alteration from "propter adulterium cum domina . . . ." The erased words are probably "de Usk priorissa." I suppose that Adam means to say that the lady was a natural sister of sir Edward Cherleton. The words "mirabiliter" and "in ipsius . . . . grates" are also written on an erasure. And "hac de causa" seems to be a correction on "acta causa."

[2] The MS. reads "Aremirandine," which may be a corruption of the name "Ilderim" (or Thunderbolt) given to Bajazet I. on account of his astonishing conquests; or, perhaps more probably, of a title compounded of amir. Walsingham and other chroniclers refer to the battle as being fought against Balsak or Bassak, a son of Bajazet, who was named "Admiratus": a title in which may be recognized the origin of our word "admiral." Bajazet was defeated and taken prisoner by Tamerlane at Angora, 28th July, 1402.

A.D. 1401. servant of the king[1], who, bearing royal letters, sought to exact for sale of such cloths, contrary to the king's promise made on his happy coming into the land, a tax, rate, or due, which had been remitted. Wherefore, because the king's justices, although peers of the realm, were unable to punish such excess, on account of the resistance of the country people, the king in his own person coming to the place settled the disturbance in some way, though with gentle punishment.

Another such tax-gatherer, at Dartmouth in the county of Devon, being attacked by the people, seized a boat and hardly got out to sea.

At Bristol, the wives, acting the part of their husbands, gave the gatherers a like rebuff, sometimes giving and receiving wounds.

The lord of the Orkney Isles[2], to the great injury of my lord of March, who was still in wardship of the king, thought good to attack Ulster in Ireland belonging to the earl.

On the feast of the Ascension of our Lord (12th May), in this year, the villeins of Bergavenny rose against their lord, the lord William Beauchamp[3], and, setting free, at the very gallows, three men condemned to death for theft, who on that same day, at the will of that second Jezebel, the lady of the place, without reverence to festival or time, were to be hanged, overwhelmed with a flight of arrows sir William Lucy, knight, who had been appointed to the execution.

On the eve of the Apostles Peter and Paul (28th June), Isabella, daughter of the king of France, queen of England and wife of Richard late king of England (though not yet

[1] His name was Thomas Newton. The riot took place rather earlier in the year.—Wylie, *Henry the Fourth*, i. 198.

[2] Apparently Henry Sinclair, second earl of Orkney. Henry, the first earl, died about 1400, but the exact date is uncertain.

[3] William Beauchamp, baron Bergavenny, married Joan, daughter of Richard Fitzalan, earl of Arundel (*ob.* 1397). She died in 1435.

eleven years of age), after much treating thereon, departed
from London to go to her father, clad in mourning weeds,
and showing a countenance of lowering and evil aspect to
king Henry, and scarce opening her lips, as she went her
way. Concerning her departure, of which I was witness,
the people were moved, and those in power chafed, some
cursing her coming into this land, as being the cause
of all its troubles, others declaring that, now she was
gone, she would bring on us greater worry by the kindling
of her vengeance for the death of king Richard, her late
husband.

In this year of our Lord 1401, on the feast of the
Commemoration of Saint Paul (30th June), a certain king
of arms of Scotland, called in English a herald, was, for
evil things spoken by him against king Henry in the
kingdom of France, condemned by the court of chivalry,
being first stripped of his badges and with his face turned
to his horse's tail, to ride through London and then to
have his tongue cut out[1]. But the king sent him back
to the king of Scotland, his master, with letters setting
forth his disgrace, in a more handsome way than that
same ride.

On the same day was a great suit in the same court
between the lord Grey of Ruthin, for whom I appeared,
and the lord Edward Hastings, for the arms: on a field
gules, a manche or, whereof above, which were formerly
those of the lords of Bergavenny; and between sir John
Colvylle of Dale[2], against whom I pleaded, and sir Walter
Byttervey, of the county of Salop, knights, for the arms:
on a field or, a fess, three torteaux in chief gules; judgement

[1] His name was Brice or Bruce. He had been seized and committed
to the Tower on the 25th May.—Wylie, *Henry the Fourth*, i. 193.

[2] Executed, in 1405, for complicity in archbishop Scrope's rising.
Shakespeare introduces him in the *Second Part of king Henry the
Fourth* (act IV. sc. iij.) as Falstaff's prisoner. An impression of his
seal of arms, with the bearings mentioned in the text, is in the
British Museum, no. xlix. 17.

of possession being refused to both sides, and they urging the suit with much heat.

All this summer, Owen Glendower, with many chieftains of Wales, who were held for exiles and traitors to the king, lurking in the mountainous and wooded parts, sometimes pillaging, sometimes slaying their foes who laid snares and attacked them, harassed with no light hand the parts of West and North Wales; and they took prisoner the lord Grey [1].

The French invaded and seized to their own use a great part of Gascony, which clave to England, and specially all the county of Perigord [2], to wit, the city itself with thirty castles and all the lands of the same county. I saw the count, on the abovesaid day, come to the king to tell him of these things.

Then also I saw some lords of Ireland who loudly complained before the king against the fierceness of the Irish mercenaries.

Tideman, bishop of Worcester, sometime monk of Hales, whose counsel I had been, and whom king Richard, after that he had been driven forth from his monastery for the evil arts of brewing charms and weaving spells, raised up to be bishop, first of Llandaff, and then of Worcester, ended his days on the sixth day of June [3]. Wherefore the king wrote to the pope on behalf of master Richard Clifford, keeper of his privy seal, that it would please him, having changed the provision of the church of Wells,—which had

---

[1] Glendower's rebellion first arose out of a quarrel with lord Grey of Ruthin. Grey was taken prisoner early in 1402, and paid 10,000 marks for his ransom.

[2] Archambaud IV., count of Perigord, was, for rebellion, deprived of his county and condemned to death, in April 1398; but the capital sentence was remitted. He fled to England at the end of the year. His son, Archambaud V., was likewise banished in the following year. The county of Perigord was given to Louis, duke of Orleans.

[3] Tideman de Winchecumb, abbot of Beaulieu, bishop of Llandaff, 5th July, 1393; translated to Worcester, 25th January, 1396.

been made to the same Richard, who however had not yet A.D. 1401. been consecrated by reason of the king withstanding it,— to make provision to him of the church of Worcester, and to master Henry Bowet, doctor of laws (with whom I had been retained), of the church of Wells, which had now been vacant for a year and a half on account of the said resistance [1].

On the same feast of Commemoration of Saint Paul (30th June), the lord George, earl of Dunbar in Scotland [2], became the liege-man of the king of England, yielding up to him all his possessions and strongholds held in the kingdom of Scotland; but it was said that the Scots, forestalling this his deed, seized the same to the use of the king of Scotland, so that such homage and surrender seemed to do but little profit, aye very little, to the king of England.

Behold!, there was sent to king Henry the following letter [3], suiting well with the times: " Most illustrious

---

[1] Richard Clifford, dean of York, bishop of Worcester, 1401; translated to London, 1407. Henry Bowet, archdeacon of Lincoln, bishop of Bath and Wells, 1401; translated to York, 1407.

[2] George, earl of Dunbar and March, renounced his homage to his king on the 25th July, 1400. He had taken offence because the duke of Rothsay, son of king Robert III., had broken a contract to marry his daughter. He returned to Scotland in 1408.

[3] This letter was addressed to Henry by Philip Repyngdon, or Repington, then abbot of the monastery of St. Mary de Pré at Leicester. Repyngdon had been an active supporter of the tenets of Wycliffe, but abjured in 1382. He was abbot of St. Mary de Pré from 1394 to 1404; chancellor of the university of Oxford in 1397, and again in 1400–1402; bishop of Lincoln, 1405–1419. He was made a cardinal by Gregory XII. in 1408. He resigned his bishopric on the 10th October, 1419; and died probably in 1424. Henry, on his accession to the throne, made Repyngdon his chaplain and confessor, and admitted him to his friendship. An interesting anecdote, illustrating their intimate relations, is told in the MS. register of the charters of Leicester abbey (Cotton MS., Vitellius F. xvij. f. 42 b), and is quoted, not quite accurately, by Tanner (*Bibliotheca*, 622). It is to the effect that, immediately after his victory at Shrewsbury, Henry sent a special messenger to Repyngdon: " Memorandum quod

prince and most serene lord, may it please your highness, with your wonted graciousness, to look favourably upon me your highness's servant, who, filled heart and soul with grief, lie prostrate at your feet. Whereas your singular serenity did require of me, the least of your servants, when last I went out from before you with heavy heart, that, if I should hear aught adverse, I should make it known unto your excellency without delay, now, as your most obedient servant, do I take my pen in my hand to show what I have heard and seen. Truly, most noble prince, as the wise Solomon doth bear witness in the Proverbs of the Holy Ghost: ' Faithful are the wounds of a friend ; but the kisses of an enemy are deceitful,' [1] therefore, as a true lover of you and of your kingdom, and, according to my strength, a faithful servant to God and to you, I have chosen, with the psalmist [2], rather to be ' a doorkeeper in the house of my God,' [3] for the truth's sake, than, with traitor Judas, to live amongst kingly pleasures and carry on my lips the kiss of flattery. Therefore, dissolved in tears, and my heart torn with wounds by reason of my grief, I declare with the prophet that ' they which call thee blessed cause thee to err, and destroy the way of thy paths.' [4] And hence, of such great desolation in the hearts of the prudent, for the disorder and tumult which they .

Henricus quartus, finito magno bello in campo Salopie et victoria habita, confestim fecit proclamacionem per totum exercitum suum si aliquis servus abbatis Leycestrie fuerit ibi. Statim venit unus servus dicti abbatis, cui rex tradidit annulum de digito suo, donans ei c. solidos, precipiendo quod cum omni festinacione pergeret ad dominum Philippum, abbatem Leycestrie, et nullo modo quiescat, donec traderet ei dictum annulum, et diceret ei quod rex vivit, habens victoriam de inimicis suis, benedictus Deus ! " The same MS. records (f. 43) Repyngdon's gift to the abbey of a small cross of gold, which had been given to him by Henry. Adam was associated with him in the enquiry at Nuneaton: above, p. 220.

[1] Prov. xxvij. 6.    [2] baptista. MS.
[3] Ps. lxxxiv. 10.
[4] Is. iij. 12. Author. vers., "they which lead thee," etc.

fear shall in short time arise in this land, never, from the A.D. 1401.
days of my youth, do I remember to have heard.  For law
and justice are banished from the realm; thefts, murders,
adulteries, fornications, extortions, oppressions of the poor,
hurts, wrongs, and much reproach, are rife; and one tyrant
will doth serve for law.  And therefore sure am I that if
the gospel of Christ be true, which saith that 'every
kingdom divided against itself is brought to desolation,'[1]
and if the words of the wise man be not foolishness, who
declareth that 'because of unrighteous dealings, injuries,
reproaches, and divers deceits, the kingdom is translated
from one people to another'[2]—if, I say, all these things do
wax unbridled in the land, and there be no man of power
in the kingdom, clerk nor knight, who, as a faithful minister
of Christ, may stand up against or heal these and other
countless offences and scorn of our God, I say, with the
faithful prophet, that the Lord God, strong and long-suffer-
ing, 'is angry with the wicked every day, and if ye turn
not, he will whet his sword; he hath bent his bow, and
made it ready.  He hath also prepared for him the instruments of death; he ordaineth his arrows against the perse-
cutors,'[3] so that, after that the manifest miracles of God
and his exceeding loving-kindnesses have in fact and deed
been despised or unheeded, he shall bring down swift and
raging vengeance upon his unthankful servants and those
who openly despise him.  But we hoped that your wonderful entry into the realm of England, which I doubt not
was the work of the hand of God, would have redeemed
Israel, and would have turned to repentance those guilty
of all those sins and wicked contempts of God, 'for the
punishment of evil-doers and for the praise of them that do
well.'[4]  But now the prudent do weep, and the froward
laugh; the widow, the fatherless, and the orphan wring
their hands; and tears flow down the cheeks of those who,

[1] Luke xj. 17.
[2] Cf. Ecclus. x. 8.
[3] Ps. vij. 11-13.
[4] 1 Pet. ij. 14.

A.D. 1401. but a little while ago, with applauding hands and praising God with one voice, went forth with the sons of Israel, on the day of Palms, to welcome Christ, and who cried aloud of you, their anointed king, as of another Christ: 'Blessed is he that cometh in the name of the Lord, our king of England!' [1] hoping for a happy reign over the land. But now 'our harp is turned to mourning,' [2] and our joy is changed into sorrow, while all evils are multiplied, and the hope of healing hath with tearful sadness gone out from the hearts of men. Therefore doth God, who is a righteous judge, as a just punishment and vengeance on the neglect and carelessness of the rulers of the land, permit the commons, like wild beasts, without rule and without reason, to sit in judgement, and to usurp, contrary to nature, the government which belongeth to those above them, and to rage like the brutes, without the balance of reason, against those who are above them, those who are equal with them, and those who are below them. And in truth, if I mistake not, well may your royal authority wax wroth at the rebellion of the people, and so sorely may your vigour and warlike fierceness be roused, that even in one province of your kingdom, perhaps, which God forbid!, some twenty thousand of your liegemen may fall by the edge of the sword, till the fury of the executors be glutted—you, who, when you came into the realm of England, did pledge yourself to God and the people to shield from their enemies all and every the dwellers in the realm, poor and rich, great and small. But not thus will the murmuring of the people cease, nor will the displeasure of our angered God; but more and more will it be roused to fury, and more and more, when the time cometh, will it rage, even to vengeance, until the law and the lawful justice of your realm shall be kept, and wrongs and unjust deeds and oppressions of the people shall be done away and blotted out,

---

[1] Matt. xxj. 9.    [2] Job xxx. 31.

and, by the upright ruling of justice, every man shall have A.D. 1401.
his own ; so that peace may first be re-established between
God and man, and thence may afterwards in deed and
in truth be had between man and his neighbour. ' For who
hath hardened himself against him, and hath prospered?'[1]
Because your sins and 'your iniquities have separated
between you and your God, and have hid his face from
you,'[2] therefore, by the just judgement of God,' as many as
have sinned without law shall also perish without law,'[3]
and they who despise the law, being convinced of the law,
shall be justified according to the law. And, according to
the blessed James, 'not the hearers of the law are just
before God, but the doers of the law shall be justified'[4];
and, on the other hand, the despisers of the law shall be
confounded, as within two years we beheld ensampled in
king Richard, as in a wonder-mirror : a thing ever to be
holden in unfailing and undying remembrance by the
whole world and for all ages to come. Therefore may my
God, the sun of justice, take away the veil from your eyes,
that you may clearly see with the eyes of your mind what,
at your happy coming into the kingdom of England, you
did vow in public and in private to a faithful God who
forgetteth not, and, further, what justice and what obedience
you have repaid to a thankworthy and gracious God, and
to the kingdom of England, for all his benefits. And if you
find aught wanting, speedily, for fear of vengeance, hasten
to repay ; and if you find aught of righteousness, give
thanks to the Lord, the giver of all good things, who
rendereth justly to every man according to his deserts.
And may the Blessed Trinity, in whose hand are the hearts
of kings and the governance of kingdoms, give to you a
teachable and a yielding heart, easily led to all good, to
fulfill with faithfulness the bounden duty of kingly rank,
and to understand in your heart and throughly, and to

[1] Job ix. 4.    [2] Isaiah lix. 2.    [3] Rom. ij. 12.
[4] Jas. i. 22; Rom. ij. 13.

A.D. 1401. heal the sufferings of your people; and may the Lord open your heart in his law and in his commandments, and stablish peace in the kingdom of England for ever and ever! Written, if it please your lordship, with a trembling heart, and with yearning love, at London, on Wednesday, the morrow of the Invention of Holy Cross (4th May), by the hand of your bedesman. Most serene prince, these things, as a true worshipper of God, and as a friend of your government, if good, and as a faithful lover and bedesman of the state and of your realm, giving freedom to my heart's thoughts, have I already spoken by the words of my mouth in your presence; and now, if it please you, I write them unto you, burning with the same desire and love, aye yearning love, 'before it come to pass, that, when it is come to pass, you might believe, and that, when the time shall come, you may remember that I spake to you, saying: When he, the Spirit of truth, is come, he will guide you into all truth; and he will shew you things to come.' [1]   Behold !, 'O greatly beloved,' [2] I yearn with love."

On the twenty-eighth day of the month of July, in the year of our Lord 1401, the aforesaid queen of England, still a child, crossed over to Calais, and there, until the first day of August next following, during the treating between our people of England and the councillors of the king of France, she stayed; and on that day she, together with her jewels and dower, was honourably received by the Frenchmen, to be sent to the king of France, her father, all the English, of either sex, being sent back to their own homes [3].

In this summer the fleets of England and France attacked each other much at sea.

---

[1] John xiv. 29 ; xvj. 4, 13.          [2] Dan. ix. 23.

[3] Isabella rested three days at Calais, and on the 31st July was conducted to Leulinghen, where, after final arrangements, she was handed over to the French commissioners.

A.D. 1401.

On the morrow of the Assumption of the Blessed Virgin (16th August), in the same year, our lord king Henry, with the peers from all parts of the realm hereunto summoned, in a great and solemn council holden at Westminster, determined that his adversaries of France and Scotland should be by him assailed in war.

In this autumn, Owen Glendower, all North Wales and Cardigan and Powis siding with him, sorely harried with fire and sword the English who dwelt in those parts, and their towns, and specially the town of Pool. Wherefore the English, invading those parts with a strong power, and utterly laying them waste and ravaging them with fire, famine, and sword, left them a desert, not even sparing children or churches, nor the monastery of Strata-florida, wherein the king himself was being lodged, and the church of which and its choir, even up to the high altar, they used as a stable, and pillaged even the patens; and they carried away into England more than a thousand children of both sexes to be their servants. Yet did the same Owen do no small hurt to the English, slaying many of them, and carrying off the arms, horses, and tents of the king's eldest son, the prince of Wales, and of other lords, which he bare away for his own behoof to the mountain fastnesses of Snowdon.

In these days, southern Wales, and in particular all the diocese of Llandaff, was at peace from every kind of trouble of invasion or defence.

Among those slain by the above inroad of the English, Llewellyn ap Griffith Vaughan, of Cayo in the county of Cardigan, a man of gentle birth and bountiful, who yearly used sixteen tuns of wine in his household, because he was well disposed to the said Owen, was, on the feast of Saint Denis (9th October), at Llandovery, in the presence of the king and his eldest son [1], and by his command, drawn, hanged, beheaded, and quartered.

[1] The words "cum filio suo primogenito" might more strictly mean

At this time, about Michaelmas, a quarter of wheat on a sudden rose in price from one noble to two, and in some parts of England to three nobles.

Throughout all Wales the strongholds were repaired in walls and ditches [1].

Died the noble lord, lord John Cherleton, lord of Powis, at his castle of Pool, on the day of Saint Luke (18th October); to whom by right of inheritance succeeded the lord Edward, his brother, a most graceful youth, lord, in right of his wife, the countess of March, of Usk and Caerleon.

The lord Thomas, the king's second son, crossed over with a great host to subdue the rebellion of the Irish [2]. So too the earl of Rutland, to withstand the invasions of the French, went over into Gascony.

The Scots, refusing to treat for peace or truce with the English, determined to begin war and defiance against them on Saint Martin's day (11th November) [3].

The commons of Cardigan, being pardoned their lives, deserted Owen, and returned, though in sore wretchedness, to their homes, being allowed to use the Welsh tongue, although its destruction had been determined on by the English, Almighty God, the King of kings, the unerring Judge of all, having mercifully ordained the recall of this decree at the prayer and cry of the oppressed.

On the morrow of All Hallows (2nd November), Owen, seeking to lay siege to Caernarvon, there, in the midst of a great host, unfurled his standard, a golden dragon on

the son of the sufferer. I think, however, that the prince of Wales is referred to. Henry was in Wales in the early part of October.

[1] One of the ordinances passed on the 22nd March, 1401, was that the defences of the castles in North Wales should be kept in repair for three years at the expense of the Welsh.

[2] Thomas Plantagenet, created earl of Albemarle and duke of Clarence in 1411, was slain at the battle of Baugé, 1421. He was appointed lieutenant of Ireland in the summer of 1401, and landed at Dublin on the 13th November, and remained in the country for two years.

[3] The date of a proposed truce, to last for a year.

a white field; but, being attacked by those within, he was
put to flight, losing three hundred of his men.

At this time, our lord the king made a levy on all the
realm for the marriage of his daughters [1].

The lords Percy, father and son, subdued with vigour the
rebellion of the Scots, slaying and taking captive a great
number.

Owen and his men cruelly harried the lordship of Ruthin,
in North Wales, and the country-side with fire and sword,
on the last day but one of January, carrying off the spoil
of the land and specially the cattle to the mountains of
Snowdon; yet did he spare much the lordship of Denbigh
and others of the earl of March, having at his beck the two
counties of Cardigan and Merioneth which were favourable
to him both for government and war.

A certain knight, called David ap Jevan Goz, of the
county of Cardigan, who for full twenty years had fought
against the Saracens with the king of Cyprus and other
Christians, being sent by the king of France to the king
of Scotland on Owen's behalf, was taken captive by English
sailors and imprisoned in the Tower of London.

Messengers of Owen, bearing letters as follows, addressed
to the king of Scotland and lords of Ireland, were taken in
Ireland and beheaded: "Most high and mighty and redoubted lord and cousin, I commend me to your most high
and royal majesty, humbly as it beseemeth me, with all
honour and reverence. Most redoubted lord and right
sovereign cousin, please it you and your most high majesty
to know that Brutus, your most noble ancestor and mine,
was the first crowned king who dwelt in this realm of

---

[1] Orders were first issued on the 1st December, 1401 (*Fœdera*, viij.
232), for the levy of an aid for the marriage of the princess Blanche
with Louis of Bavaria, which took place on the 6th July, 1402.
Negotiations were also being carried on during the year and afterwards for the marriage of Henry's second daughter, Philippa, with
Eric, king of Denmark, whom, however, she did not marry till
August, 1406.

A.D. 1401. England, which of old times was called Great Britain. The which Brutus begat three sons, to wit: Albanact, Locrine, and Camber. From which same Albanact you are descended in direct line. And the issue of the same Camber reigned royally down to Cadwalladar, who was the last crowned king of my people, and from whom I, your simple cousin, am descended in direct line; and after whose decease I and my ancestors and all my said people have been, and are still, under the tyranny and bondage of mine and your mortal foes the Saxons; whereof you, most redoubted lord and right sovereign cousin, have good knowledge. And from this tyranny and bondage the prophecy saith that I shall be delivered by the aid and succour of your royal majesty. But, most redoubted lord and sovereign cousin, I make grievous plaint to your royal majesty and right sovereign cousinship, that it faileth me much in men at arms. Wherefore, most redoubted lord and right sovereign cousin, I humbly beseech you, kneeling upon my knees, that it may please your royal majesty to send unto me a certain number of men at arms who may aid me and may withstand, with God's help, mine and your foes aforesaid; having regard, most redoubted lord and right sovereign cousin, to the chastisement of this mischief and of all the many past mischiefs which I and my said ancestors of Wales have suffered at the hands of mine and your mortal foes aforesaid. Being well assured, most redoubted lord and right sovereign cousin, that it shall be that, all the days of my life, I shall be bounden to do service and pleasure to your said royal majesty and to repay you. And in that I cannot send unto you all my businesses in writing, I despatch these present bearers fully informed in all things, to whom may it please you to give faith and credence in what they shall say unto you by word of mouth. From my court. Most redoubted lord and right sovereign cousin, may the Almighty Lord have you in his keeping."

A.D. 1401.

" Greeting and fullness of love, most dread lord and right
trusty cousin. Be it known unto you that a great discord
or war hath arisen between us and our and your deadly
foes, the Saxons: which war we have manfully waged now
for nearly two years past, and which, too, we purport and
hope henceforth to wage and to bring to a good and effec-
tual end, by the grace of God our Saviour, and by your
help and countenance. But, seeing that it is commonly
reported by the prophecy that, before we can have the
upper hand in this behalf, you and yours, our well-beloved
cousins in Ireland, must stretch forth hereto a helping
hand; therefore, most dread lord and right trusty cousin,
with heart and soul we pray you that of your horsemen
and footmen, for the succour of us and our people who
now this long while are oppressed by our said foes and
yours, as well as to oppose the treacherous and deceitful
will of those same our foes, you do despatch unto us as
many as you shall conveniently and honourably be able,
saving in all things your honourable estate, as quickly as
may seem good unto you, bearing in mind our sore need.
Delay not to do this, by the love we bear you and as we
put our trust in you, although we be unknown to your
dread person, seeing that, most dread lord and cousin, so
long as we shall be able to wage manfully this war in our
borders, as doubtless is clear unto you, you and all the
other chieftains of your parts of Ireland will in the mean
time have welcome peace and calm repose. And because,
my lord cousin, the bearers of these presents shall make
things known unto you more fully by word of mouth, may
it please you to give credence unto them in all things which
they shall say unto you on our behalf, and, as it may be
your will, to confide, in full trust, unto them whatsoever,
dread lord and cousin, we your poor cousin may do.
Dread lord and cousin, may the Almighty preserve your reverence and lordship in long life and good fortune. Written
in North Wales, on the twenty-ninth day of November."

A.D 1402.    And now, O God, Thou, who of thine unbounded grace
didst grant me to fulfill my student's time at Oxford and
the three years' doctor's course, and then seven years'
service as pleader in the court of Canterbury, be it honour
or be it profit, and in all other my businesses whatsoever
hast been my help, from the days of my youth up even to
old age and decay, forsake me not; but make of me an
ensample for goodness, that they who come nigh me may
behold and be astonished, "because Thou, Lord, hast holpen
me and comforted me [1]." And now grant that my journey
to Rome, as Thou hast ordered it, both in my going thither
and in my return hither according to my desire, whether
I be numbered among advocates or auditors, may mercifully receive Thy consolation, to the honour and praise
of Thy name, and to my welfare in either man, and with
threefold honour and temporal wealth.

To be short.  On the nineteenth day of February, in the
year of our Lord 1401-2, I, the writer of this history, as,
by the will of God, I determined, took ship at Billingsgate
in London, and with a favouring wind crossed the sea, and,
within the space of a day landing at Bergen-op-Zoom, in
Brabant, the country which I sought, I set my face towards
Rome.  Thence passing through Diest, Maastricht, Aachen,
Cologne, Bonn, Coblentz, Worms, Speyer, Strassburg, Brei-
sach, Basel, Bern [2], Lucerne and its wonderful lake, Mont
St. Gotthard and the hermitage on its summit, where I was
drawn in an ox-waggon half dead with cold and with mine
eyes blindfold lest I should see the dangers of the pass, on
the eve of Palm Sunday (18th March) I arrived at Bellin-
zona in Lombardy.  Thence through Como, Milan, Piacenza,
Borgo-San-Donnino, Pontremoli, Carrara [3], Pietrasanta, Pisa,

---

[1] Ps. lxxxvj. 17.

[2] The MS. places Bern after Lucerne.

[3] The MS. reads "Carenciam," and the name precedes Pontremoli
in Adam's list.  But I have no doubt that Carrara is meant, that city
being the first important place at which the traveller would arrive on
descending from the hills towards the coast.

A.D. 1402.

Siena, and Viterbo, turning aside from Bologna, Florence, and Perugia, on account of the raging wars and sieges of the duke of Milan, of whom hereafter, and the perils thereof, and halting for two days at every best inn for refreshment of myself and men, and still more of my horses, on the fifth day of April, by the favour of God and the fear of our archer-guards, I came safely through all to Rome. And within a fortnight after being presented, with his recommendation, by the lord Balthasar, cardinal deacon of the title of Saint Eustace, who was afterwards pope John the twenty-third [1], to our lord the pope Boniface the ninth, by whom I was honourably received to the kiss of foot and hand and cheek; and then by him being given over to the cardinal of Bologna, afterwards pope Innocent the seventh [2], to be straitly examined as to my knowledge, and being approved, I was raised within a fortnight, by the counsel of the pope and the Rota, to the dignity of papal chaplain and auditor of the apostolic palace and judge of city and world, being invested by the pope himself with the ensigns of office, to wit, the cope and rochet and hat. And, within a se'nnight after, the pope assigned thirty great causes, which had been referred to his hearing, to be determined by me.

In my journey hither, first at Cologne and thence right up to Pisa mentioned above, as well by night as by day, I beheld a dreadful comet which went before the sun, a terror to the world—to the clergy which is the sun thereof, and to the knighthood which is its moon—which forecast the death of the duke of Milan, as it soon after came to pass. His dreaded arms too, a serpent azure swallowing a naked man gules, on a field argent, were then ofttimes seen in the air.

---

[1] Cardinal Balthasar Cossa became pope John XXIII. in 1410.

[2] Cosimo dei Migliorati, appointed bishop of Bologna, but refused by the people. He, however, always kept the title of cardinal of Bologna. He became pope Innocent VII. in 1404.

A.D. 1401-2.     The duke of Bavaria, being chosen emperor, entered
Italy, eagerly striving to make for Rome for his coronation.
But suffering defeat at the hands of the said duke at Padua,
his design was brought to naught, and he went back confounded into his own country [1].

A.D. 1402.     This duke, having subdued Bologna, the delight of the
world and the glory of Italy, a man before whom all the
earth was quiet [2], and who, drawing away the mighty river
Po through the midst of mountains and over many miles
of land, just as the great Cyrus turned aside the Euphrates
from Babylon, had gained Padua, died stricken by a sudden
plague, to the great sorrow of strangers, because, ruling his
lands with a rod of iron, he made passage through them
safe to wayfarers. And surely was it believed that, had
he but lived another year, he had reigned over Germany
and Italy as one kingdom. In every prince's family in
Europe he had spies in his pay, to make known to him
any news, at much cost, besides bribing the princes them-

[1] The emperor Rupert advanced into Italy against the duke of
Milan, but was beaten at Brescia, 24th October, 1401, and retired in
the following April.

[2] 1 Maccabees i. 3. Gian-Galeazzo Visconti, duke of Milan, who
succeeded his father Galeazzo in 1378. By his wonderful powers of
organization he conquered the greater part of northern Italy, and was
only checked when he came in contact with the republic of Florence.
He was almost always successful. Even when attacked on all sides by
a combination of his enemies, he shook them off and advanced to
fresh victories. His last conquest was Bologna. Soon after its capture,
the appearance of the plague frightened him into retirement at
Marignano, where however he sickened and died on the 3rd September, 1402. He is said to have pointed to the comet which was then
blazing in the heavens as a sign of his approaching end. Adam has
made some mistakes in details. Padua was taken by Gian-Galeazzo
as far back as 1388, but whether the waters of the Brenta (not the
Po, as Adam states) were diverted does not appear. However, the
duke had the design, which he partly carried out, of changing the
channels of the Brenta and Mincio and drying up the lagoons of
Venice, in order to attack the republic. In 1390, Padua was re-
covered by Francesco da Carrara, who effected an entry by the bed of
the river.

selves to his side by great gifts. But see !, according to
the common saying, "Ill-gotten gains scarce reach the third
generation," his great-uncle, the archbishop of Milan [1], a
man of large mind, vicar of the empire, leaving, at the
time of his death, his two nephews, that is, the lord
Galeazzo, father of this duke, and the lord Bernabo, his
uncle, captains in the emperor's camp, bequeathed to them
pride and mutual hate by filching the rights of the empire,
and left his ill-gotten gains to be rooted out in the person
of this duke who was the third after him.

The said duke of Milan being dead, the duke of Bavaria
who was elected emperor sent a solemn embassy to the
pope for his confirmation; which he had, as appears below.

Bologna, Perugia, and other lands of the church, which
had been commended to the deceased duke, broke into
revolt; but they were brought back into subjection by the
diligence of the said cardinal of Saint Eustace.

Throughout all Lombardy and Tuscany treaties of peace
and concord were torn up; and, by the party-warfare of
Guelphs and Ghibellines, tumults raged with fire and sword.

On the twenty-second day of December, abuses of indul-
gences, unions, exceptions, pluralities, and other things
which brought scandal on the court, were, while I was
present, revoked [2]; or more truly I may say they were
renewed; for, alas !, a new sale of reinstatements of what
had been revoked grew up. Contrary to the revocation

---

[1] This was Giovanni Visconti, the friend of Petrarch, who governed
Milan from 1349 to 1354. He recalled his three nephews, Matteo,
Galeazzo, and Bernabo, from exile, and on his death left them to
divide his possessions. He was not vicar of the empire, as Adam
states; but that office was held by his father Matteo. So far from
quarrelling, as the chronicle would make out, Galeazzo and Bernabo,
the two despots, after murdering their brother Matteo, seem to
have governed the Milanese with remarkable amiability towards one
another.

[2] The bull is recited in *Annales Ric. II. et Hen. IV.* (Rolls
series), 351.

A.D. 1402. of unions, the pope conferred on me, the writer of this history, the archdeaconry of Buckingham, together with the churches of Knoyle, Tisbury, and Deverill, in England; but, the Welsh war preventing this, he gave me the archdeaconries of Llandaff and Caermarthen, together with the church of Llandefailog and the prebend of Llanbister.

A.D. 1403. In the year of our Lord 1402-3 Ladislas, king of Naples, seeking for himself the kingdom of Hungary, by right of descent, entered into it with a strong force. But having subdued only Slavonia, he was bravely driven back by Sigismund, brother of queen Ann of England and afterwards emperor, who then held the kingdom; and he returned with shame into Italy [1].

My God!, how grievously now are church and empire harassed and laid waste with internecine slaughters, the one with two, the other with three rulers. And specially that empire of the Greeks—founded by the race of the great Constantine, who ruled in Britain, the son of the holy Helena, and first by him transferred from the Romans to the Greeks, and lastly by pope Stephen from the Greeks to the Germans—is now, as all men know, laid waste by Turks and Tartars.

A.D. 1402. On the day of Saint Alban (22nd June), near to Knighton in Wales, was a hard battle fought between the English under sir Edmund Mortimer [2] and the Welsh under Owen Glendower, with woeful slaughter even to eight thousand souls, the victory being with Owen. And, alas!, my lord the said sir Edmund, whose father, the lord of Usk, gave me an exhibition at the schools, was by fortune of war carried away captive. And, being by his enemies in England stripped of all his goods and hindered from paying ransom, in order to escape more easily the pains of captivity, he is known by common report to have

---

[1] Ladislas, king of Naples, was crowned king of Hungary, 5th August, 1403; but was defeated and retired to Naples in October.

[2] Uncle of the earl of March.

wedded the daughter of the same Owen; by whom he had a son, Lionel, and three daughters, all of whom, except one daughter, along with their mother are now dead. At last, being by the English host beleaguered in the castle of Harlech, he brought his days of sorrow to an end, his wonderful deeds being to this day told at the feast in song.

In this year also the lord Grey of Ruthin, being taken captive by the same Owen, with the slaughter of two thousand of his men, was shut up in prison; but he was set free on payment of ransom of sixteen thousand pounds in gold [1].

Concerning such an ill-starred blow given by Owen to the English rule, when I think thereon, my heart trembles. For, backed by a following of thirty thousand men issuing from their lairs, throughout Wales and its marches he overthrew the castles, among which were Usk, Caerleon, and Newport, and fired the towns. In short, like a second Assyrian, the rod of God's anger [2], he did deeds of unheard-of cruelty with fire and sword.

These things I heard of in Rome. And there everything was bought and sold, so that benefices were given not for desert, but to the highest bidder. Whence, every man who had wealth and was greedy for empty glory, kept his money in the merchants' bank ready to further his advancement. And therefore, as, when under the Old Testament the priesthood were corrupted with venality, the three miracles ceased, to wit, the unquenchable fire of the priesthood, the sweet smell of sacrifice which offendeth not, and the smoke which ever riseth up, so I fear will it come to pass under the New Testament. And methinks the danger standeth daily knocking at the very doors of the church.

In this year the king, with one hundred thousand men and more divided into three bodies, invaded Wales in war

---

[1] See above, p. 230.     [2] Isa. x. 5.

A.D. 1402. against Owen. But he and his poor wretches keeping close in their caves and woods, the king laid waste the land and returned victoriously, with a countless spoil of cattle, into his own country.

The lord Fitz-Walter, who while he was in Rome listened to my advice (but in this he consulted me not), wishing to pass by sea from Rome to Naples, was taken by Saracens and carried prisoner to Tunis, the chief city of the savages; but, though ransomed by Genoese merchants, he delayed returning to England by reason of the troubles there and died in Venice [1].

A.D. 1403. For the abovesaid confirmation of the emperor, this text is pronounced: "Father, glorify thy son." [2] And the pope answers in the form of a collation [3]: "Mine arm also shall strengthen him." [4] And this is the bull of confirmation: "Boniface, bishop, servant of the servants of God, to our well-beloved son, Rupert, duke of Bavaria, king elect of the Romans, greeting and apostolic blessing. The most high Father of boundless majesty, who disposeth all things by His merciful providence, hath ordered the world in kingdoms, which He hath willed to be directed by good counsel and to be governed with healthful governance, lest the estate of the human creature, which doth manifest the image and likeness of his Creator, might be overwhelmed in the gulf of the stormy waves of this world, or hindered from the sweetness of its peace,—yea, verily, that all might live a peaceful life bound by the rule of law and honour, and that each one might abstain from offence against his neighbour, and might acknowledge with natural love the great Maker, might worship Him when known, and might submit to His dread empire. At length the Father, looking down from on high, and seeing that the people which He

---

[1] Walter, ninth baron Fitz-Walter, died in 1407.
[2] John xvij. 1.
[3] After "collacionis" the manuscript reads "in utroque," of which I can make nothing.          [4] Ps. lxxxix. 21.

had made had incurred the sentence of damnation, merci- fully sent into the world the King of Peace, His only begotten Son, our Lord Jesus Christ, for the salvation of His people. Who, putting on the flesh of our mortality, rescued the people from the pangs of everlasting death and redeemed them with His precious blood. We therefore, who, undeserving though we be, bear His office in this earthly kingdom, like unto a shepherd keep watch both of body and mind, in order that we may see what may be profitable to the flock committed to us, and what toil must be spent, so that, with the support of Him, whose are the pillars of the earth [1], and by whom actions are weighed [2], and who governeth the deeds of mortal men, we may profitably make manifest our part in that office, to attain those things which we see of necessity to be of advantage to the faithful. In truth, of late, the pope Urban the sixth of blessed memory, who was next before us, perceiving by prudent thought that the world is placed by the bonds of sin in evil plight, and that, by the ordering of the Lord, to whom all things are obedient, the mother church of Rome doth hold the chief lordship over kings and kingdoms, as mother and mistress of all, in order that by her ministry the foundation of the catholic faith may be profitably governed, did by divers messages and letters, at various times, with fatherly affection urge our well-beloved son in Christ, Wenceslaus, then king of Bohemia and of the Romans, for the defence of the church militant and for the honour and estate of the holy empire, as his duty re- quired of him, to come to the parts of Italy in order to receive the crown of the empire. And seeing him to be lukewarm herein from too much sloth, while he still warned him now by letters, now by messengers, he most urgently required the electors of the empire, as the principal members thereof, with fitting means and remedies to exhort the same Wenceslaus to come down into Italy, and with earnestness

[1] 1 Sam. ij. 8.     [2] 1 Sam. ij. 3.

and with due warnings to enforce him thereto. But at length the same Urban, our predecessor, by the Lord's will, was withdrawn from the light of this life, and we, being by the mercy of God raised up to the summit of the most high apostleship, burning with mighty zeal of heart, sought to withstand the offences which we saw ever growing up to the harm of the church of Rome, our spouse, and to the harm, too, of the empire; and therefore, as well by messages as by letters, with fatherly kindness we interposed our part, in divers ways which we thought fitting, in order that we might induce the said Wenceslaus to such journey, never giving up any possible chance which appeared serviceable. And, perceiving that the exhortations of our said predecessor and our own profit nothing, in order that the prudence of the apostolic court should leave nothing untried in so grave a case and weighty a matter, we bring to remembrance that ofttimes we have written to our reverend brethren and beloved sons, the electors of the sacred empire, that they—having regard to the dangers which from the exceeding sloth of the aforesaid Wenceslaus were ever assailing the church and the empire and the Christian religion, and above all seeing that France, which we ever perceive to strain with all her strength for the usurpation, or at least for the division, of the church and empire, hath seized on the imperial city of Genoa, which lieth in the very jaws of Italy—should in all fitting ways and with timely remedies and warnings, rouse up the same Wenceslaus to come into Italy, after the manner of the lords his predecessors, in order to receive from our hands the crown of the empire, and to prevent the French from making good their footing in Italy, and also to defend the church and empire as by his office he is bound to do. At length, the electors themselves perceiving that his delay did cause endless losses, and that the abovesaid exhortations were in vain and of none effect, though made with persistence for this matter which is so sacred and necessary

for Christendom, and that the same Wenceslaus was utterly
useless for the government of the said empire, and lest
the commonwealth of the same empire should by his
idleness fall to pieces, they took care to make known to
us by their envoy that, diligently enquiring into the slothfulness of the aforesaid Wenceslaus, whereby a crop of dangers
has sprung up to the world, they had made ready, after
setting him aside, to proceed to the election of another
who might cope with those evils; and, although the
deposition of the same Wenceslaus is acknowledged
altogether to pertain to us, yet, armed with our authority,
they with one accord did proceed to the deposition of the
same Wenceslaus, and with one accord did choose thee,
our well-beloved son, duke of Bavaria, count-palatine and
co-elector of the Rhine, to be king of the Romans and next
emperor. And thou, after duly considering this matter,
and urged by them and others, hast given thy free consent
to such election. And afterwards, by a solemn embassy
on thy behalf, it was humbly prayed of us that we, of our
wonted kindness, would deign to approve by apostolic
authority the setting aside of the same Wenceslaus and
thy election and whatsoever followed thereon, and to
decree and pronounce thy person to be fit and proper to
undertake the aforesaid dignity of imperial exaltation.
Therefore, being credibly informed of all the aforesaid
matters, and of thy person, as far as in thine absence it
might be, and of thy virtuous conduct and qualities and
of the allegiance whereof thou art approved towards us
and the Roman church, and having weighed carefully all
these things with our brethren, the cardinals of the holy
Roman church, listening to thy prayer, and with their
consent, to the praise and glory of God, and the glory of
the Virgin Mary and of the blessed Apostles Peter and
Paul, and the honour of the said Roman church, and the
good and profit of the holy empire, and the good estate
of the world, seeing that difficulties and dangers are likely

to arise from the carelessness of the said Wenceslaus, and holding as valid and according to our will his deposition and thy election and whatsoever thereupon followed, we receive thee as the chosen son of us and of the church, and, granting to thee grace and favour and considering thy person to be fitting, we pronounce and choose thee to be king of the Romans, declaring thee to be fit therefor, and decreeing the anointment and consecration and the crown of the empire to be bestowed on thee by our own hands; making good every defect, which in any way in such election might be found, of our sure knowledge and fullness of apostolic power. And we enjoin all faithful and liege men of the empire, of what estate soever they be, even though they be pre-eminent in kingly or priestly honours, that they most fully obey and look towards thee as king of the Romans and emperor elect. Let no man therefore, etc. Given at Rome, at St. Peter's, on the first day of October, in the fourteenth year of our pontificate."

In the next year, on behalf of the crown of England claimed for the earl of March, as is said, a deadly quarrel arose between the king and the house of Percy of Northumberland, as kin to the same earl, to the great agitation of the realm as it took part with one side or the other; and a field being pitched for the morrow of Saint Mary Magdalene (23rd July), the king, by advice of the earl of Dunbar of Scotland, because the father of the lord Henry Percy and Owen Glendower were then about to come against the king with a great host, anticipating the appointed day, brought on a most fearful battle against the said lord Henry and the lord Thomas Percy, then earl of Worcester. And, after that there had fallen on either side in most bloody slaughter to the number of sixteen thousand men, in the field of Berwick [1] (where the king afterwards founded a hospice for the souls of those who

---

[1] Berwick was the village where Hotspur passed the night before the battle of Shrewsbury.

there fell) two miles from Shrewsbury, on the eve of the
said feast, victory declared for the king who had thus
made the onslaught.   In this battle the said lord Percy,
the flower and glory of the chivalry of Christendom, fell,
alas!, and with him his uncle.   Whereby is the prophecy
fulfilled: "The cast-off beast shall carry away the two
horns of the moon." [1]   There fell also two noble knights
in the king's armour, each made conspicuous as though
a second king, having been placed for the king's safety
in the rear line of battle.   Whereat the earl of Douglas
of Scotland, then being in the field with the said lord
Henry, as his captive, when he heard victory shouted for
king Henry, cried in wonder: "Have I not slain two king
Henries (meaning the said knights) with mine own hand?
'Tis an evil hour for us that a third yet lives to be our
victor." [2]

The circuits of full indulgence [at Rome], to lighten the
heavy toil of visiting others, consist in seven churches,
to wit: St. John Lateran, St. Mary the greater, St. Cross of
Jerusalem, St. Peter's, St. Paul's, St. Lawrence without the
walls, and SS. Fabian and Sebastian.   Also, since it would
be too much labour to visit all places of indulgence in the
church of St. Peter, it sufficeth to visit within the circuit

---

[1] The application of the "two horns of the moon" to the two
Percys who fell is no doubt suggested by the Percy badge, a crescent.
See a memorandum in Nicolas, *Acts of the Privy Council*, i. 209, in
which the Percy retainers are described at this very time as wearing
the badge: "et pluseurs chivachent devers lui, leur cressans as
braas."

[2] "This battell lasted three long houres, with indifferent fortune
on both parts, till at length, the king crieng Saint George! victorie!
brake the arraie of his enemies, and adventured so farre, that (as some
write) the earle Dowglas strake him downe, and at that instant
slue sir Walter Blunt, and three other, apparelled in the king's sute
and clothing, saieng: I marvell to see so many kings thus suddenlie
arise one in the necke of an other."—Holinshed, iij. 26.   "Another
king! they grow like Hydra's heads." — Shakespeare's *Hen. IV.*,
*pt. I.*, act V. sc. iv.

seven altars, to wit: the high altar of Saint Peter, wherein he lieth, as too Saint Paul doth in the high altar of his church, although their heads are in St. John Lateran, adorned with gold; also the altars of Saint Cross, Saint Veronica, Saint Gregory, Saint Fabian and Saint Sebastian, Saint Leo pope, and Saint Andrew.

Also, in the city there are four patriarchal churches, to wit: St. John Lateran, which is the mother of city and world, wherein also is the papal throne, and out of regard to which the pope is called Roman pontiff, once the palace of the great Constantine, and by him given for this purpose to Saint Silvester, but first built by Nero; the second, St. Mary the greater; the third and fourth, St. Peter's and St. Paul's; and in these churches all the cardinals, as canons thereof, receive their titles, and at their high altars no man doth celebrate save only the pope. Yet there are in the city many other churches, as in the line :—

" In Rome are chapels a thousand six hundred and five."

From one of my fellow auditors of the Rota, a native of Naples, I heard that in these days a certain ship of that city was taken by the Saracens, wherein was a lady of noble birth, who, choosing death rather than suffer violation, on a sudden cast herself into the sea and was drowned.

After the above-told battle between the king and the said lord Henry Percy, Owen with his manikins, issuing from his caves and woods and seizing his chance, marched through Wales with a great power as far as the sea of the Severn, and brought into subjection with fire and sword all who made resistance and also those beyond the same sea wherever the Welsh, as such, had been pillaged by the country people, sparing not even churches; whereby at last he came to ruin. And then with a vast spoil he retired for safety to the northern parts of Wales, whence are spread all the ills of Wales, and to the mountains of Snowdon, amid smothered curses on his open adulteries.

The men of Bristol with an armed fleet, under their A.D. 1403.
captains, James Clyfford and William Rye, esquires, invaded
the parts of Glamorgan, and pillaged the church of Llandaff;
but, being beaten by the country people, through a miracle
of Saint Theliau, they were driven back in disorder with
no small loss.

The prior of Launde and sir Roger Clarendon, knight, A.D. 1402.
natural brother of king Richard, and eleven of the order
of grey friars, doctors in theology, who were confederates
of the said Owen [1], being betrayed to the king by their own
fellows, at Tyburn in London were drawn and hanged with
cruelty. And many lords and ladies, even countesses, were
for the same cause committed to prison.

The king, hoping to receive help through her, took to A.D. 1403.
wife the widow of the duke of Brittany and sister of the
king of Navarre [2]. But straight his hopes were rendered
vain, for the Bretons, denouncing the marriage, along with
the French and under command of the count marshal of
Aquitaine and the lord of Huguevilles of Normandy, entered
Wales in great force to the succour and support of Owen ;
and wasting all the march with fire and sword they did no
small hurt to the English [3].

[1] The charge against them was that of spreading the rumour that
Richard was still living, and so attempting an insurrection against
Henry ; and also of sending money to Owen.

[2] Henry's marriage with Joan, daughter of Charles of Navarre and
widow of John Montfort, duke of Brittany, was celebrated on the 7th
February, 1403.

[3] The Bretons made a descent on the southern coast and burned
Plymouth, in 1403. The following year they reappeared near Port-
land and did some damage, but were beaten off with the loss of their
leader (Walsingham, ij. 259, 261). Owen Glendower entered into an
offensive and defensive alliance with the French on the 14th June,
1404. In consequence of this, an expedition of one hundred and
forty sail, with 12,000 men, sailed from France to Wales, under
command of Jean, sire de Rieux et Rochefort, marshal of France and
Brittany (the count marshal of Aquitaine, of the text above), and
Jean, sire de Hangest, lord of Avenescourt and Huguevilles, grand-
master of the crossbows.

A.D. 1402,
1406.

The king bestowed his two daughters in marriage, the one to the king of Denmark, and the other to the son of the duke of Bavaria, emperor elect as above, with no small taxation of the kingdom [1].

A.D. 1402.

The house of Percy, short time before its ill fate as told above, in battle at Homildon Hill in the march of Scotland, slew many thousands of the Scots; and many nobles, amongst whom was the Douglas spoken of above, were carried off captive by the fortune of war. And it is believed that from this victory that house became too much puffed up, and, according to the common saying: "An haughty spirit goeth before a fall," [2] went headlong to its ruin. And no wonder; for it is not the saw which cutteth the log nor the axe which cleaveth, but the hand of man. So the hand of God alone giveth the victory.

A.D. 1404.

In these days the church of Hereford being vacant [3], the pope made disposition thereof in favour of me the writer of this history, but through the envy of the English who opposed me and by letters belied me with poisonous words to the king,—whereby for four years long, an exile, on sea and land I suffered the pangs of grievous misfortunes [4],—I got not advancement but rather abasement, and suffered the last degree of poverty, stripped of benefices and goods, and, like Joseph, hearing among strangers a tongue which I knew not, albeit I was paid with gold for my counsel.

Meanwhile in England many parliaments were holden, wherein both more stringent statutes were passed against papal provisions, and more than was wont the clergy and people were taxed with heavier levies. And no marvel; for

---

[1] Blanche, married to Louis of Bavaria, son of the emperor, in 1402; and Philippa, married to Eric of Denmark, in 1406.

[2] Prov. xvj. 18.

[3] By the death of John Trevenant on the 6th April, who was succeeded by Robert Mascall on the 2nd July, 1404.

[4] Adam was in exile for six years in all, from 1402 to 1408. He is here taking account of the last four years, dating from 1404, the year in which he is writing.

they were pressed to hold their own in war against France, A.D. 1404. Scotland, Ireland, Wales, and Flanders, and owing to war they had lost sixty thousand pounds which Wales was accustomed to pay.

Owen and his hill-men, even in their misery, at Machynlleth, usurping the right of conquest and other marks of royalty, albeit to his own confusion, held, or counterfeited or made pretence of holding parliaments.

The earl of Northumberland, father of the above famous lord Henry, at the prayer and request of all the parliament, was shortly, though to no purpose, reconciled to the king. And in this parliament, a certain villein, Serle by name, was for the murder of the duke of Gloucester, of whom above, drawn, hanged, disembowelled, beheaded, and quartered [1].

On account of the slanders of mine enemies, I, the present writer, sent unto the king, under mine own hand, although to no purpose, the following letter, which was delivered to him by the bishop of Salisbury [2]: "With most humble and devout recommendations and with continual prayers to God for the health of your royal majesty. Most excellent and most benign prince, whereas, after leave had of your royal highness to visit the court of Rome, I with others did so visit it, it did please our father and lord in Christ, Boniface, by the divine will pope, that now is, to attach me, although unworthy, to the college of the lords auditors of his sacred palace. And I, trusting in Him who can make the rough places smooth and who alone can water with the spring of His grace the heart which is parched, and hoping that He would make fruitful my short-coming with the dew of His loving-kindness, did accept that unpaid office,

[1] William Serle, a devoted servant of Richard II., was taken prisoner on the northern border and brought to Pontefract. He was executed with more than ordinary cruelty, suffering "more and severer penalties than other our traitors have endured before these times."—Wylie, *Henry the Fourth*, i. 450.

[2] Richard Metford, translated from Chichester, 1395; died, 1407.

A.D. 1404. to the praise of God and that I might do more useful service to your royal pre-eminence and to your servants; and I now hold the same; and still for some time, if fortune favour me in the cost of my sojourn here, I, as best I can, by the help of divine favour, do purpose to practise it, offering myself with heart and soul to your royal wishes and commands, whereunto, according to the small measure of my littleness, I am ready ever to do service; praying in most humble and devoted wise of your royal majesty, under the shadow of which I live and move (seeing that nothing is so acceptable to me as the safe estate, and the happy progress, and the glorious triumph thereof), that, graciously bearing in the memory of your royal loving-kindness how I grieved for your absence which was caused by the shafts of envy, as my lord your brother[1] knoweth (to whom I foretold your prosperous return, just as it happened, at which happy fortune I rejoiced—as I hope hath not been hid from your royal goodness—and wherein I as a sharer gave most loyally at mine own expense my service, poor as it was, till you had right worthily been exalted to the pinnacle of royal majesty), of your charity your majesty may please to restore me to the old age of my insignificance with the relief of some better promotion. This offering of me your humble and faithful bedesman and willing servant may your majesty be pleased to accept with your inborn clemency and graciousness, inclining not the ears of your loving-kindness to those who speak evil of me, but favourably deigning to foster me and my fortunes and my friends under the shadow and protection of your exalted arm; and may He, by whom all kings and princes are governed, grant you to triumph over your foes, at your desire, and to reign long and happily here on earth, and hereafter to pass to the heavenly kingdom. Written at Rome, in the fifth year of your reign, on the twelfth day of the month of September."

[1] No doubt Henry Beaufort, then bishop of Lincoln, the king's half-brother.

On the feast of Saint Michael (29th September) there came, A.D. 1404. seeking for the union of the church, a solemn embassy, on the part of the kings of France, Castille, and Aragon, and of other princes who were obedient unto him who sat at Avignon[1], to pope Boniface; and he gave them public audience. And the bishop of St. Pons[2] in France spake to him in these words, not acknowledging him as pope: "Most dread lord, if you of yourself do not feel pity for the souls of others, yet my lord doth offer himself as ready to lay down his life to find a way of union." Whereat lord Boniface burst forth: "Thy lord is false, schismatic, and very antichrist." "Saving your reverence, father, not so. My lord is holy, just, true, catholic; and he sits upon the true seat of Saint Peter"; and further the same bishop cried out with heat: "Nor is he simoniac." Whereupon Boniface, astonished at these words, withdrew into his chamber, and within two days (1st October) was plucked out from this life. Concerning this matter, on the same night, I had two dreams. The first was, that I beheld Saint Peter, robed in his bishop's vestments, sitting without his gate, and he cast forth to earth another who appeared as a pope, of sad countenance and foul, and who was sitting on his left hand. In the second, there appeared unto me a fox chased by dogs, which, taking the water, seized in his mouth, to keep himself afloat, a branch of willow which grew above, and lay covered to the nostrils; and, when he was again hunted out by the dogs, in terror he left the water, and, as a last refuge, ran into a hole, where forthwith he disappeared. Whence I understood that the fox, though ever greedy, yet ever remaineth thin; and so Boniface, though gorged with simony, yet to his dying day was never filled.

A certain German also showed me a letter sent from other parts by the hands of a holy man, wherein he declared

---

[1] Benedict XIII.

[2] Pierre de Rabat, bishop of St. Pons de Tomières, in the province of Narbonne, 1397–1409.

that he had seen Saint Michael fell Boniface to the earth with a heavy buffet; and so, on his festival, it came to pass as above.

By the death of our lord the pope the safe-conduct of the ambassadors became void; and so they were by the captain of the castle of Sant' Angelo therein thrust prisoners.

For the election of a new pontiff of Rome the cardinals entered the conclave, which was entrusted to the safe keeping of the king of Naples and six thousand of his soldiers.

The pestilent Roman people rose divided into the two parties of Guelphs and Ghibellines, and for the space of three weeks with slaughter and robbery and murder did they harry each other, either party urging the creation of a pope on its own side; yet by reason of the said guard could they not come near to the palace of Saint Peter nor to the conclave. And so their partisanship brought about the election, as pope, of one who lay not in the bosom of either party, namely Innocent the seventh, a native of Sulmona [1]. And, when his election was made known, the Romans attacked his hospice, and, after their greedy fashion, nay rather from festering corruptness, they sacked it, leaving therein not so much as the bars of the windows [2].

The conclave is a close-built place, without anything to divide it, and it is set apart to the cardinals for the election of the future pope; and it must be shut and walled in on all sides, so that, excepting a small wicket for entrance which is closed up after they have gone in, it shall remain strongly guarded. And therein is a small

[1] Cosimo dei Migliorati, elected on the 17th October. Adam is mistaken in saying that the king of Naples was in Rome. He had been called in by the people, and was marching on the city when the conclave met. The cardinals hastened to make the election before his arrival.

[2] This seems to have been the custom of the times. At a later period a guard was set over the house of the pope elect.

window for food to be passed in to the cardinals, at their
own cost, which is fitted so as to open or shut as required.
And the cardinals have each a small cell on different floors,
for sleep and rest; and three rooms alone in common, the
privy, the chapel, and the place of election. After the
first three days, while they are there, they have but one
dish of meat or fish daily, and after five days thence bread
and wine only, until they agree.

Heavens! The glory of Cæsar and Augustus, of Solomon
and Alexander, of Ahasuerus and Darius, and of the great
Constantine—where is it now? And whither shall this
glory pass? Let it be left to the outcome of the future!

> " Proud he wears the triple crown
>     Whose vassals throng his foot to kiss;
> For king or kaiser's angry frown
>     Not a wight cares aught, I wis.
> Christ his pardon freely gave,
>     Gave his grace without a price;
> He, who here will favour have,
>     To mammon's god must sacrifice."

Christ was meek, and his vicar a lowly fisherman. But
Plato bids me hold my peace.

Such advancement of my lord Innocent saw I thus in
a vision, how he went up from the sacristy of St. Peter's
to the altar to celebrate mass, robed in the papal vestments
of scarlet silk woven with gold.

The dead pope, after the proclamation of the election, was
carried to the church of St. Peter for the funeral rites, which
lasted for nine days.

A disgraceful treaty (for how soon was it broken!) was
made with the Romans by the new pope, to wit, that, the
lordship of the city with the borough of St. Peter and the
castle of Sant' Angelo and yearly tribute of six thousand
florins being reserved to him, as well as the appointment
of the senator, who, however, must be born a full hundred

A.D. 1404. miles from Rome, the rest should remain at the will and behoof of the people [1].

The aforesaid king of Naples, having received from the pope Campania and the sea-coast for a yearly tribute for five years, afterwards a cause of weariness to the church, departed with his army from Rome.

On the feast of Saint Martin (11th November) the new pope went down from the palace to the church of St. Peter for the ceremony of his coronation, and at the altar of St. Gregory, the auditors bringing the vestments, he was robed for the mass. And, at the moment of his coming forth from the chapel of St. Gregory, the clerk of his chapel, bearing a long rod on the end of which was fixed some tow, cried aloud as he set it aflame: "Holy father, thus passeth away the glory of the world"; and again, in the middle of the procession, with a louder voice, thus twice: "Holy father! Most holy father!"; and a third time, on arriving at the altar of St. Peter, thrice: "Holy father! Holy father! Holy father!" at his loudest; and forthwith each time is the tow quenched. Just as in the coronation of the emperor, in the very noontide of his glory, stones of every kind and colour, worked with all the cunning of the craft, are wont to be presented to him by the stone-cutters, with these words: "Most excellent prince, of what kind of stones wilt thou that thy tomb be made?" Also, the new pope, the mass being ended by him, ascends a lofty stage, made for this purpose, and there he is solemnly crowned with the triple golden crown by the cardinal of Ostia as dean of the college. The first crown betokens power in temporal things; the second, fatherhood in things spiritual; the third, grandeur in things of heaven. And after-

---

[1] The local rivalry between the pope and the people of Rome was temporarily settled to the advantage of the former in 1393, when, on condition of his coming to reside in Rome, Boniface was allowed a certain share in the municipal government of the city. But this arrangement soon broke down, and there ensued constant quarrels between pope and people, as told by Adam.

wards, still robed in the same white vestments, he, as well A.D. 1404.
as all the prelates likewise in albs, rides thence through
Rome to the church of St. John Lateran, the cathedral seat
proper of the pope. Then, after turning aside, out of
abhorrence of pope Joan, whose image with her son stands
in stone in the direct road near St. Clement's, the pope,
dismounting from his horse, enters the Lateran for his
enthronement. And there he is seated in a chair of porphyry, which is pierced beneath for this purpose, that one
of the younger cardinals may make proof of his sex ; and
then, while a "Te deum" is chanted, he is borne to the
high altar [1].

[1] A detailed account of the papal coronation will be found in the
*Tableau de la Cour de Rome*, par le Sieur J. A[imon] (1726), and in
*Cérémonies et Coutumes Religieuses* (Amsterd. 1723). Interesting particulars of the coronation of Innocent VIII., in 1484, are given by
Burchard (*Diarium*, Florent. 1854), which may be compared with
the narrative in our text. Burchard himself, as chamberlain, performed the ceremony of lighting and extinguishing the tow. At
a later time this simple emblem of the "gloria mundi" was changed
for a more elaborate one, the fragments of tow giving place to
miniature models of castles and palaces made of that material. Part
of the ceremonies were, however, omitted in Innocent's coronation
for the following reason. It appears that if the pope rode in state
up to the Lateran, the people claimed both horse and baldacchino.
To resist this claim, and to avoid the rudeness of the crowd, Innocent
dismounted near St. Clement's church and was thence carried in
a chair. But this only made matters worse ; for the pressure of the
crowd was so great that his bearers, making a rush to carry him
through, were swept right into the church, so that "pontificis
receptio in ostio sive porticu Lateranensi et ejus locatio in sede
stercoraria ac jactio pecuniarum fieri non potuerunt," and the procession reached the high altar in ludicrous confusion.

The ceremony of the "sedes stercoraria," with the meaning given
to it in this and other chronicles, is discussed by the editor of
Burchard's Diary (48 sqq.), who quotes from various authorities
to show that the name arose from the verse chanted by the cardinals,
as they raised the pope from the chair in which he was seated within
the portico of the church : "Suscitat de pulvere egenum et de *stercore*
erigit pauperem" (Ps. cxij. 7) ; and that by an obvious confusion the
chair became in the popular mind a "sedes probatoria."

For an account of pope Joan (whom our chronicler, curiously

In their street the Jews offered to him their law, that is the Old Testament, seeking his confirmation; and the pope took it gently in his hands, for by it we have come to the knowledge of the Son of God and to our faith, and thus answered: "Your law is good; but ye understand it not, for old things are passed away, and all things are become new[1]." And, as if for a reproach, since they being hardened in error understand it not, he delivers it back to them over his left shoulder, neither annulling nor confirming it[2].

There rode with the pope not only those of his court and the clergy, but also the thirteen quarters of the city with their captains and standards at their heads. During the progress, in order to ease the thronging of the people, largess was thrice cast among the crowd, and a passage was thus cleared while it was being gathered up.

Now I rejoice that I was present and served in that great solemnity, as also I did in the coronation of king Henry the fourth of England and in the confirmation of the empire spoken of above.

O God!, how much is Rome to be pitied! For, once thronged with princes and their palaces, now a place of hovels, thieves, wolves, worms, full of desert places, how pitifully is she laid waste by her own citizens who rend each other in pieces! Thou, O Rome, didst draw thine origin from Æneas after the Trojan war, as my nation too

enough, calls Agnes), see Burchard's Diary, 82 sqq. Niem, who was contemporary with Adam of Usk, states in his *Historiæ sui temporis* that her image stood in the street between the church of St. Clement and the Coliseum.

[1] 2 Cor. v. 17.

[2] This curious custom is traced back to the twelfth century, when, on Innocent II. taking refuge in France and entering Paris, the Jews presented him with a copy of their law (*Cérémonies*, etc., I. pt. i. 81). Burchard (47) says that in his time the ceremony took place at the Monte Giordano, but formerly near the castle of Sant' Angelo, from whence, however, the Jews were driven by the insults of the people. In later times (*Cérémonies*, etc., I. pt. ij. 59) the scene was removed to the Coliseum.

from his great-grandson [1]; whence we stand on common ground in affliction. And truly it was first her empire which devoured the world with the sword, and next her priesthood with mummery. Whence the lines :—

" The Roman bites at all ; and those he cannot bite he
    hates.
Of rich he hears the call ; but 'gainst the poor he shuts
    his gates."

And it was thus that a certain German spake who was pleading before me for a benefice, but whose cause was sold by forestalling the date in the papal camera :—

" Weep, pitiful Rome, for thy fame past recall ;
  ' No man shall sell !,' but Rome chaffers for all.
  Thus shalt thou pass away, thus shalt thou fall."

The church of London being vacant, the college of auditors with one accord went up and besought the pope to translate thither the lord Guy de Mona, bishop of St. David's, and to make provision of the church of St. David's to me, the writer of this history [2]. Which thing was very pleasing to him, and he said : " We thank you heartily that you have thus recommended him to us ; and we rejoice at so good an occasion of making provision for him of a better church in his own country, for the church is one of dignity. And we knew his good estate, and also the same Guy de Mona at the time when we were collector in England." But, the matter being noised abroad, my enemies with mighty clamour and speech declared against it to the king and cardinals who held benefices in England, threatening the latter that, if they should allow this thing, they would lose their benefices by the king's displeasure ; and they swore

---

[1] The mythical Brut.

[2] Robert de Braybrooke, bishop of London, died on the 27th August, 1404. He was succeeded by the ex-archbishop, Roger Walden, dean of York. Guy de Mona remained bishop of St. David's till his death in 1407.

A.D. 1404.   that the king would send me to prison and the gallows. Moreover they forbade the merchants to lend me money, under pain of expelling their partners out of England. And this was the chief hindrance of the matter; and so it fell to the ground.

On Christmas day I was present at the papal mass and the banquet, as also on other festivals, together with others my fellow auditors and officers. And, in the first mass, at the right horn of the altar was placed a sword adorned with gold, bearing on its upright point a cap with two labels like a bishop's mitre, for this purpose: that the emperor, if present, holding the naked sword, should himself read, as deacon, as having been anointed, the gospel: "There went out a decree from Cæsar," [1] and should have the same sword from the pope for himself. But, owing to the absence of the emperor, a cardinal deacon read the gospel, and the pope delivered the sword to the count of Malepella [2], as being the most noble then present [3]. In the same mass, double gospel and epistle are read, in Latin by two Latins, and in Greek by two Greeks,

[1] Luke ij. 1.

[2] This name is not to be identified. Probably the scribe has blundered. Count Ugo Balzani, *La storia di Roma nella cronica di Adamo da Usk*, 1880, has found a certain count Manopello, of the Orsini faction; but his identity with "Malepella" must remain uncertain.

[3] So also Burchard (81), under date of 1486, has the following: —"Feria secunda, 25 mensis Decembris, festo Nativitatis Domini Dei Salvatoris Nostri Jesu Christi, Papa processionaliter venit sub baldachino ad basilicam S. Petri, praelatis et Cardinalibus post crucem praecedentibus. Dominus Sinulphus clericus Camerae ad sinistram Crucis ensem cum pileo portavit super altare majus in cornu epistolae, ubi per totam missam mansit. Qua finita, Sanctissimus Dominus Noster, sedens in sede solii, comiti Tondillae ante se genuflexo tradidit gladium cum capello, dicens sine libro: *Accipe gladium, et sis defensor fidei et Sanctae Romanae Ecclesiae, in nomine Patris, etc.*, quem ille accipiens osculatus est manum, deinde pedem Papae, et dedit eum uni ex suis militibus, qui eum continuo ante ipsum portavit." The *Table de la Cour de Rome* (348) gives the following

for their satisfaction, because they say that they were driven out of the church.

The pope created a noble Roman knight prior of the Hospital of Saint John, his own marshal girding him with the sword; but the pope, after drawing the sword, only struck him with the hand on the forehead, saying: "Bear this blow for the commonwealth and faith of Christ." Then the new knight kisses the other knights standing round about, and is robed by the pope's hand in the tunic of religion; and by the pope's order the golden spurs are fastened on his heels by another knight.

Two monks from India, black and bearded, do reverence to the pope, and, in proof of their belief in Christ, they show the crosses which they bear upon their breasts, and their baptism on the right ear, not made with water but with fire, saying: "From the time when the sound of the apostles of Jesus Christ went out into all the earth [1], and specially from the time of Saint Thomas, our apostle, although others have turned aside from the faith, never have we so turned aside, but we are true Christians." And they had a gracious hearing [2].

account of the origin of this ceremony: "Les Papes fondent cet usage sur ce qu'on trouve dans le second livre de Machabées, au chapitre xv., où il est dit que Judas Machabée étant prêt à combattre Nicanor, général de l'armée d'Antiochus, Roi de Syrie, eût une vision en laquelle il lui sembloit voir le grand Prêtre Onias, quoique mort, qui prioit Dieu pour le peuple Juif, et le Prophète Jeremie qui présentoit au même Judas une epée dorée, en lui disant ces paroles: Reçois cette sainte epée que Dieu te donne et avec laquelle tu detruiras les adversaires de mon peuple Israël." The cap was usually sent to some prince or captain distinguished by his zeal for the church. Pius II. sent a sword and cap to Louis XI.

[1] Rom. x. 18.

[2] These two "nigerrimi barbati" seem to have been Ethiopians. Marco Polo (ed. Yule, 2nd edit. 1875, ij. 421) in his account of Abash, or Abyssinia, thus refers to the custom of branding: "The Christians in this country bear three marks on the face; one from the forehead to the middle of the nose, and one on either cheek. These marks are made with a hot iron, and form part of their baptism; for, after

I, the writer of this history, delivered to the pope the following petition: "Holy father, in the town or borough of Usk, in the diocese of Llandaff, is a certain most honourable monastery of a prioress and convent of nuns, under the profession of the order of Saint Benedict, who serve God with the greatest devoutness, which was of old sufficiently endowed with possessions, rents, and other profits; and in this monastery none but virgins of noble birth were and are wont to be received. But now, owing to the burnings, spoilings, and other misfortunes which have been caused by the wars which raged in those parts, or otherwise, this same monastery hath come to such want that, unless ready help be forthwith found by your holiness, the sisterhood will be forced to beg for food and clothing, straying through the country, or to stay in the private houses of friends; whereby it is feared that scandals may belike arise. And, seeing that within the walls of the same monastery there is built a certain chapel in honour of Saint Radegund, virgin nun, once queen of France, where-

that they are baptized with water, these three marks are made, partly as a token of gentility, and partly as the completion of their baptism. There are also Jews in the country, and these bear two marks, one on either cheek; and the Saracens have but one, to wit, on the forehead, extending halfway down the nose." Colonel Yule, in his learned note upon the passage, refers to the early mention by Matthew Paris, under the year 1237, of the practice among the Jacobite Christians of branding their children on the forehead before baptism. It appears also to have been the custom in Abyssinia and other parts of Africa to cauterize the temples of children, to inure them against colds. Ariosto, referring to the emperor of Ethiopia, has:

"Gli è, s'io non piglio errore, in questo loco
Ove al battesmo loro usano il fuoco."

Salt, the traveller, mentions that most of the people of Dixan had a cross branded on the breast, right arm, or forehead; which he explains as a mark of attachment to the ancient metropolitan church of Axum. And in Marino Sanudo it is stated that "some of the Jacobites and Syrians who had crosses branded on them said this was done for the destruction of the pagans, and out of reverence to the Holy Rood."

unto the men of that country bear great reverence, and which they ofttimes, and specially at the feasts of Easter and Whitsuntide, are wont to visit; now therefore, prayeth your holiness your faithful chaplain and auditor of causes of the sacred palace apostolic, who first drew breath in the same town or borough, and of whose blood are some of the same sisterhood, that, having pity with fatherly compassion on that monastery and prioress and nuns, you will deign graciously to grant to all Christian people who, so often as, on the second days of the said festivals, for all time to come, they shall visit the same chapel, shall stretch forth the hand of help thereto, some indulgence, as your holiness shall think fit, with necessary and proper clauses, as in form." And the pope signed it thus: "So be it, as it is asked," for five years and as many periods of forty days, as appeareth in the same chapel.

Being lodged near the palace of St. Peter, I watched the habits of the wolves and dogs, often rising at night to this end. For, while the watch-dogs barked in the gateways of their masters' houses, the wolves carried off the smaller dogs from the midst of the larger ones, and although, when thus seized, the dogs, hoping to be defended by their larger companions, howled the more, yet the latter never stirred from their posts, though their barking waxed louder. And so I pondered on the same sort of league which we know doth exist in our parts between the great men of the country and the exiles of the woods.

The viper race of Lombardy, split up into Guelphs and Ghibellines, with plundering and fire and slaughter, and even eating the flesh of the dead and dashing against rocks their own offspring if they took the opposite side, destroyed each other and certain of their cities at this time.

The Romans, about Quinquagesima Sunday, meet together for public games, with the captains of their different quarters, in a large well-equipped body; and, according to the words of Saint Paul: "They which run in a race run

A.D. 1404. all,"[1] they strive manfully for the prize. They set up three large silver rings, tied to a rope up aloft, and, galloping past them on their horses, they hurl lances through them, to carry them off as prizes. At these games are present the senator of the city, the two wardens, and the seven regents, in state dress, the block and axe being borne before them for the punishment of the mutinous. In the same games, too, the Romans run riot like brute beasts in drunkenness (the feast of misery), with unbridled extravagance, like to the sons of Belial and Belphegor.

Then, on the same Sunday, at the cost of the Jews, four carts covered with scarlet cloth, in which are eight live boars, being placed on the top of the mountain of all the earth (which is so called because it is made of earth brought thither from all parts of the world in token of universal lordship)[2], are yoked with eight wild bulls; and, they being shaken open by the swift descent downhill and the beasts set free, the whole becomes the prey of the people. And then every man pell-mell rushes at the beasts with his weapon; and, if it so happen that any one brings not home to his wife some part of the spoil, he is accounted a poor spirit and a craven who shall not have her company till the feast of Saint Pancras. And often in the scuffle they cut down or wound in particular the courtiers whom they hate for wrongs done to wives and daughters.

After this, they set up on the points of spears three cloths, one of gold for the best horses, and another of silver for the

[1] 1 Cor. ix. 24.

[2] The Monte Testaccio, an artificial mound of some size, measuring in circumference at the base about half a mile, situated near the Tiber, to the south of the Aventine. It was the rubbish-heap of the Romans, which began to accumulate, it is thought, about the beginning of the empire. It consists almost entirely of broken pottery, chiefly of vessels used in the importation of products from the provinces and mostly from Spain. The adjoining landing stages were apparently cleared periodically of broken or waste vessels, which were discharged on to this site.

second best, and the third of silk for the swiftest mares; A.D. 1404. and whichever horseman severally reaches them first in the races takes them as prizes.

At length, after the onslaught on the beasts, some with shreds, others with the guts or filth on their sword-points, they depart in sorry procession home to their wives.

On the feast of the Purification (2nd February) the pope blesses candles, and, seated on his throne, he gives them out, not only to each there present, but also to all the catholic princes and princesses of the world, greater or smaller according to the differences of state and rank. They are made of white virgin wax. So too on Ash Wednesday, in his own person, he distributes ashes to all present. And of all this I was witness; for I received the candles for the king and queen of England, and I held the bason of cinders for the pope.

On my first coming to Rome, I heard of a certain prophet, who falsely gave himself out to be Elias and that he was sent on earth by God the Father to beget His son Christ; and that he had spurned Christ with his foot as He bare the cross to His crucifixion; and he declared that that woman, who should be thought worthy to be gotten with child by him and to conceive the Christ, should be blessed for ever and ever and should have the true glory which was assigned to the false Mary. But, carrying on his rites and services in secret places and corners, he cunningly kept himself out of light. And so it came about that Roman ladies visited him with eagerness to lie with him, feeding him with all sorts of dainties. But at last he was found out by the Romans, and dragged out of hiding, and carried away to the Capitol; where, after confessing that he had dishonoured more than a hundred Roman ladies, wives, widows, and virgins, (and he had done the same at Venice,) he was burned.

On the (fourth) Sunday in mid-Lent, in which is chanted "Lætare Hierusalem," for relief of Lent now half-spent, the

A.D. 1404. pope at mass bears in his hand a rose [1] of great price, cunningly wrought of gold and silver, and anointed with myrrh and balsam whereby it gives forth sweet perfume through all the church, and after mass he gives it to the most noble knight there present; who, with his friends then gathered together in his honour, afterwards rides forth on the same day in full state, bearing it in his hand [2].

On behalf of the emperor of Constantinople, a solemn embassy came to the pope, declaring that they had been wrongfully bereft of the Roman empire, which was due to them as sprung from the person of the great Constantine, but which was wickedly usurped by the tyrant of Germany; and they prayed him that it be given back, with the kingdom of Naples and all Lombardy, or that otherwise a day and field be by him appointed to either side, in front of the city, to fight for this claim. The pope answered that, because of their heresies and schisms, and mostly for that concerning the Holy Ghost, whom they affirm to proceed from the Father alone and not from the Son, and because they make not oral confession, and put leaven in the bread, therefore were they righteously bereft of that same empire. Moreover, he added with a smile: "We seek not to have to do with the shedding of Christian blood."

From these Greeks I learned that the princes of Greece were fully descended from the said Constantine and his three uncles, Trehern, Llewellyn, and Meric, and from other thirty thousand Britons who were carried thither from Britain with him; and that such men of British race, in token of their blood and lordship, bear axes in their country, which others do not [3]. I learned further that

---

[1] The MS. reads "rosarium."

[2] The rose is sent to a princess or a favourite church. The institution of the ceremony is attributed to Urban V., who sent a rose in 1366 to Joan, queen of Sicily.—*Cérémonies*, etc., ij. 15.

[3] The Warangian guards are evidently here referred to. This body of men has been represented as formed from English, Celtic, or German recruits. "With their broad and double-edged battle-axes

their empire is almost worn out by the attacks of Turks A.D. 1404.
and Tartars—just as the land of the Britons, the land of
their origin, was laid waste by the Saxons, as all men
know.

On Palm Sunday, the pope has palms and branches
blessed, and afterwards, as above said of the candles, he
also distributes the same, which are sent abroad altogether
at the cost of the Genoese; but, failing the palms, olive-
branches are given, at least to those there present. But the
pope himself bears aloft two palm-branches and two branches
filled with dates, of a great weight, in support whereof two
knights attend him.

On Holy Thursday, the pope mixes the oil and chrism,
and after mass, outside the gate of St. Peter, with the
greatest solemnity he goes up on a raised scaffold and, in
the vestments of the mass, glittering with gold and precious
stones, he blesses the people. And from thence, the
veronica being first seen, the pilgrims in a thronging crowd
depart with joyful hearts.

At the last, he excommunicates by name the anti-pope
along with his cardinals and favourers, and all heretics,
schismatics, pirates, and brigands, and those who hinder
the free passage of pilgrims and of provision (and above
all that for the palace apostolic) to Rome [1]. And herefor
he himself and all the cardinals hold in their hands white

on their shoulders, they attended the Greek emperor to the temple,
the senate and the hippodrome; he slept and feasted under their
trusty guard; and the keys of the palace, the treasury, and the
capital, were held by the firm and faithful hands of the Warangians "
(Gibbon, *Decline and Fall*, ch. lv.). There was a great migration of
Englishmen to the East after the Norman invasion, and "among the
Englishmen who at various times during William's reign sought
fresh homes in foreign lands, not a few made their way to the New
Rome, and there, in the service of the Eastern Emperors, they not
uncommonly had the satisfaction of meeting the kinsmen of their
conquerors in open battle " (Freeman, *Norman Conquest*, iv. 627).

[1] For example, in 1398, Onorato, count of Fondi, in his quarrel
with Boniface IX., had seized Ostia and cut off the supplies.

A.D. 1404. waxen candles, and, when the excommunication is finished, they cast them among the people with the final words: "So be it! So be it!"

At length, after the banquet, he washes the feet of his guests, giving to each one two groats[1]; the which money his servants receive again from them who had it, for that in this behalf they carry them on their shoulders to the pope.

On Easter Day the office of the pope differs but little from the office of other days, save that he allots one share of the Host to his sub-deacon, and another share to his deacon, and the third share to himself in communion; and turning his face to the people, he sucks and draws up the Blood through a long golden tube, decked in the middle with the arms of the king of Aragon. The arms of the same king have also other two privileges in the court, by reason of benefits of his ancestors: for letters of grace, as it is known, are adorned with silken threads in the colours of the said arms; and the pope's canopy too has its yellow and red colours[2]. But after the banquet, holding converse in his chamber with his guests, he sits upon his throne, and he gives bountifully and dispenses with his own hands ginger and pepper, in token of the pepper which was exchanged between Darius the great and Alexander the great[3].

On the Saturday in Easter the pope celebrates mass in albs, and, just as above said of the candles and the palms,

---

[1] The *grossus* or Italian "grozzo," a silver coin of four "danari." It was on this coin that the English groat of fourpence was based in 1351.

[2] Innocent VII. was a Neapolitan.

[3] It was not pepper that was exchanged between Darius and Alexander. Adam, as usual, knows only half the story. The fable tells us that Darius sent to Alexander some sesame seed, as typical of the multitude of his troops. Alexander replied that the seed was numerous but tasteless, and, as typical of his own troops, sent mustard seed to Darius, who found it small but pungent.

he distributes consecrated *Agnus Dei* [1] of white wax; and
I held the bason [2], which was emptied many times, and I had
for myself those that were left at the end. And as to this
*Agnus*, here are verses :—

> " Of balm and cleansèd wax and chrism distilled
>   This Lamb is made, a gift with power fulfilled :
>   The Fountain's Child, whom mysteries express,
>   It guards the labouring mother in her stress.
>   From lightning flash, from things malign it saves ;
>   The chaste who bear it do not fear the waves.
>   It stifles sin, as erst the blood of Christ.
>   The good find gifts. E'en fire may not resist.
>   From sudden death it shields, from Satan's woe ;
>   Who honours it shall triumph o'er the Foe."

Master Richard Scrope, now approved a saint by reason of
countless miracles, archbishop of York, of England primate,
and of the apostolic see legate, as well as that most seemly
youth and illustrious, the earl of Nottingham, marshal of
England, because that, as it was declared, they were rebels
to the king, were beheaded at York [3]. The citizens of
York, lying naked to their drawers on the ground, as if

---

[1] Cakes of wax stamped with the *Agnus Dei.*

[2] The bason in which the *Agnus Dei* were placed and presented to
the pope for distribution. " Chaque pape, la première année de son
pontificat, et puis de sept ans en sept ans, a coutume la semaine dans
l'octave de Pâques de bénir solennellement les *Agnus Dei*, qui sont
de petits pains de cire blanche, ronds, tant soit peu elliptiques ou
ovales, moulés en forme de médailles, où il y a d'un côté la figure de
Jésus-Christ ressuscité, moulée sous celle d'un agneau qui tient
l'étendard de la Croix, et de l'autre part il y a sur le revers quelque
saint en demi-relief, qui est ordinairement ou le patron particulier du
pape régnant, à sçavoir celui qui porte son nom de baptême, ou celui
pour lequel il a le plus de dévotion, et dont il croit l'intercession
plus efficace auprès de Dieu."—*Tableau de la Cour de Rome*, 355.

[3] Archbishop Scrope and Thomas Mowbray, earl marshal and earl
of Nottingham, joined the rising of the earl of Northumberland and
lord Bardolf, whose fate is described afterwards ; they were beheaded
at York on the 8th June, 1405.

a second Day of Judgement were come, on account of their favour shown in this behalf, sued and had the king's pardon.

On the seventh day of August, fourteen chief citizens of Rome, for that in the consistory they scoffed at the pope and his deeds, were slaughtered by his nephew, captain of the men at arms, as they were going away, at San Spirito [1]. Wherefore the Romans, to the number of three hundred thousand, rose in fury, shouting death to the pope and to all his courtiers and to foreigners. Forthwith fled the pope, along with his men at arms, to Viterbo. Those who stay behind are slaughtered, or cast into prison and robbed. And that day was to me, the writer of this history, a day of wrath and of calamity and of misery, for that, being stripped even to my shoe-latchets, I hardly escaped their tyranny with my life, lying hid for eight days in the garb of the friars preachers.

The Romans, with trumpets going before, acclaim the pope a traitor and a hypocrite, and reverse his arms in the streets, and paint a picture of him head downwards with the devil bringing him the crown. Forthwith the king of Naples with his Ghibellines and his army seized the city. By help and favour of a certain Roman, I, like the beggar that I was, (for a merchant had fled with my moneys at the first report,) in company with sailors, and

---

[1] On the death of Boniface IX. on the 1st October, 1404, and the subsequent election of Innocent VII., Ladislas, king of Naples, who had befriended Boniface, reconciled the Romans to the new pontiff, but with an ulterior view to his own advantage. Quarrelling recommenced in the next year. On the 2nd August, 1405, the citizens attempted to wrest possession of the Ponte Molle from the papal troops, but they were repulsed with loss. Negotiations were then opened, and on the 6th of the month a deputation of the Romans waited on the pope. On their way back they were decoyed by the pope's nephew, Ludovico, marquis of Ancona, into the hospital of San Spirito, and eleven of them were massacred. The people rose, and Innocent fled from Rome on the evening of the same day.—Creighton, *History of the Papacy* (1897), ij. 188.

even as one of them, passing by way of the Tiber and
Ostia and the city of Albano, (where Brutus, grandson
of Æneas and first king of the Britons, was born,)
through Corneto, came to the pope at Viterbo, telling
him all. Wherefore, jeering at me, he used to say:
"Get thee back to thy mates, and don thy sailor's garb
again !"

On the feast of the Epiphany (6th January) the wretched
Romans, being oppressed by the said king, sent the keys
of the city to the pope, promising to him full dominion
over the city.

I, the writer of this history, was poisoned at Viterbo by
the dart of the envious; wherefore, swooning away seven
times, I was laid out for dead; and, by reason of the
thieving of the Romans and the flight of the merchants,
as I have told above, my friends too going their way when
my goods went theirs, for a season I was bereft of the
means of life. But, under the order of the pope, the
poison was found out in my turbid urine by a certain
Jew, the pope's physician, Helias by name; and after
much suffering and cost, blessed be God!, my health was
renewed. And according to the word of the Lord: "Adam
the man is become as one of us,"[1] I was restored to the
Rota among the coauditors.

At Rome, meanwhile, in the palace of St. Peter and
on the papal throne sat John of Colonna, chief patron of
the Ghibellines and ruthless delegate of the above-named
king, and thrust out his feet to be kissed and shrank not
from doing other unheard-of things in mockery of the pope.
And therefore the pope sent forth to Rome, against the
tyranny of the king and this John, a great host under
Paul Orsini, his captain[2]. And so, the followers of the
king taking to flight, the blockade was raised and the
invasion crushed.

---

[1] Gen. iij. 22.          [2] On the 26th August, 1405.

The pope with his court went back Romewards[1]; and, according to the line:

> "For, in sooth, the scarlet cope
> Marketh death for thee, O pope";

and again:

> "Of justice that is fair in thee
> May the white horse token be!"

he has four white chargers of state for his saddle-horses, trapped with gold and precious stones and red silk. On one he sits; and three follow, mounted by nobles. The canopy with the arms of the king of Aragon is borne aloft on spear-points above him. He is robed in a very wide cape, aye, of exceeding width, of bright scarlet, the borders whereof are held spread out by four running footmen, so that the horse cannot be seen; and all round about him is overshadowed. He is girt about the breast above the stole and the rochet, which is very fine. There are four broad hats, with cords of cunning and precious workmanship, of red silk, whereof he wears one on his head; and the other three are set upon three stands on three horses sumptuously trapped, the cords of the same being knotted and reaching to the ground on either side of the necks of the horses, which are ridden by three nobles, who go before in company with the pope; and thereto other things of pomp unheard of by men and greatly to be wondered at. There follows him on a great white horse a chair for sitting, for mounting, for dismounting, and for withdrawing for the needs of nature, fitted with a fixed ladder or steps. Boys with olive branches meet him, crying "Hosanna!" Many things hath mine eye seen, but greater than these hath not mine ear heard[2]. And in truth I, the writer of this history, many times communed with myself by the way.

There was argued before me in the palace apostolic the

---

[1] Innocent returned to Rome on the 13th March, and lived there quietly till his death, 6th November, 1406.        [2] Job xiij. 1.

case of and concerning the monastery of Saint Mary of Scotland at Vienna in Germany [1]. Marvelling whence the Scots had to do with that, I enquired and had it thus :— By reason of the pestilent teaching of Mahomet, religion both public and private throughout all Germany being quenched, and afterwards by Charles the great being restored among the people, Saint Columcille [2] was brought out of Ireland, because the faith failed not there, for the instruction and edification of the princes, and he restored and built up again the religion of private men. Whence, in all the chief places throughout Germany, monasteries of the Scots (now called the Irish) are known as cells subject to the monasteries of Ireland, (late called Scotland after Scota, the daughter of Pharaoh,) and held in the profession of Scottish, now Irish, saints, who were sent over hither to this intent. And surely, as to the change of name : is it not from those same Scots coming into Britain that the name of Albany was changed and called, after them, Scotland ? Is it not from the Britons occupying Armorica that the name was changed and the land is now called Brittany ? And so from the Angles, England, from the Hiberi, Hibernia or Ireland, are borrowed names. And thus passeth the glory of the world !

Among other miracles of this Saint Columcille, who lies buried together with Saint Patrick and Saint Bridget in Down in Ulster, is this : invocation of his name being uttered, and at the same time being written down and cast into the flames, overcomes fire. Whence the verses :—

> " Saint Columba, with thy name
> Quench the mischief of the flame ! "

and

> " Grant, Columba, my desire ;
> Keep this roof-tree safe from fire ! "

[1] The Schottenkloster, founded in 1158.

[2] It is scarcely necessary to say that Saint Columba was never in Germany ; and to make him contemporary with Charlemagne is too absurd.

A.D. 1406. These then, as of origin Scots out of Egypt, after the passage of the children of Israel through the Red Sea, seeing that the plagues of God smote them, forsook their native soil, and dwelled under the king of Spain in the Basque country. But, being accused to the king, and in token of their treason having had their clothes cut in front, and being accused a second time and having had them cut behind also, they were expelled as traitors, with their garments thus shorn, in the time of Gurguint Brabtruc, king of the Britons, the founder of Canterbury and son of the great Belin, who, being on his way home from Norway, from collecting tribute, granted to them Ireland, which was then untilled, to be held of him [1].

Certain nobles of Ireland (in whom I trust not, but rather in Saint Patrick) declared to me, at the time when I was procuring high promotions for them, that after the said passage the Scots served the children of Israel in the desert, and above all by bringing away the brazen serpent. But, because they differed in faith, they were driven away, and went down into the Basque country, as above said ; and for such service they were rewarded by the God of the children of Israel, and to this day are free from noisome snakes.

A.D. 1412. From a certain chaplain of the diocese of Bangor, returned back from the Holy Land, I had it that he with other five hundred pilgrims, being driven by stress of weather at sea within the dominion of the soldan of Babylon, was cast into prison and held captive for the space of a year. But, the soldan having been conquered meanwhile

---

[1] Adam would find both in Geoffrey of Monmouth and in Giraldus Cambrensis the story of the colonization of Ireland by the Scots, whom king Gurguint Brabtruc, on his way home from subjugating the rebellious Danes, met just arrived in their ships from Spain at the Orkney Isles. But it does not appear whence he got the episode of the shorn garments. See *Galfredi Monumetensis Hist. Britonum* (ed. Giles), 49; and *Giraldi Cambrensis Topographia Hibernica* (Rolls series), dist. iij. cap. viij.

in a stricken field by the king of Damascus and beheaded, A.D. 1412.
the new soldan summoned those same pilgrims before his p. 103.
judgement-seat, who for mercy cast themselves down before
him; and he smote with violence on the judgement-seat
two strokes with a naked sword which he bare in his hand,
but a third blow with gentleness and graciously, in token
of pity and forbearance—otherwise they had all been dead
men—and he spake thus: "Let the men of Genoa, along
with all those of France and Spain, seeing that they are of
their league, be led back to prison, to pay ransom as re-
prisal, because three ships of their people have plundered us.
But let all the other Christians be let go free, for I would
gladly with justice show favour to all Christians." And
thus the chaplain went forth free [1].

On the feast of Saint Barnabas (11th June), being im- A.D. 1406.
poverished by disbursements, as I have told above, and on
account of the thanklessness of friends, as I shall tell below,
I departed from the court; and I journeyed through Siena,
Genoa, the marquisate of Montferrat, Asti, Moncalieri, and
Susa, and, on the feast of the blessed Peter and Paul
(29th June), over the Mont Cenis, almost perished with

---

[1] Adam has here anticipated an event which happened in the year
1412. He must have met the Bangor chaplain after his return home
to Wales, and not, as one would suppose from his narrative, while he
was abroad. The "soldan of Babylon" or sultan of Egypt into whose
power the chaplain fell was Nasir Faraj, of the Mamluk dynasty of
sultans who governed Egypt from the middle of the thirteenth century
to the early part of the fifteenth century. In 1412 he was defeated
by the amir Shaykh el Mahmudi, governor of Damascus, and was
executed on the 28th of May of that year. The caliph Musta'in was
temporarily made sultan, and was the "new soldan" spoken of in the
text. He was of the line of Abbasid caliphs, of the second branch,
who took refuge in Egypt in the thirteenth century and remained
under the protection of the sultans until the conquest of Egypt by
the Turks in 1517. European pirates had raided the coasts of Egypt
and Syria in the early years of the fifteenth century.—See Deguignes,
*Hist. générale des Huns* (1756), p. 331; Jarrett, *Hist. of the Caliphs*
(1881), p. 534; and S. L. Poole, *The Mohammadan Dynasties* (1894),
pp. 80–83, and *Hist. of Egypt in the Middle Ages* (1901), p. 333.

A.D. 1406.  the cold, and through Savoy by way of Lans-le-bourg and
Aiguebelle; in which town I saw formally emblazoned in
a hostel the arms of the lord Lionel, duke of Clarence, the
second born of England, and of the other nobles who came
with him out of England to his marriage with the daughter
of the lord Galeazzo, lord of Lombardy [1].

A.D. 1405.    On the feast of Saint Gregory (12th March), Griffith,
eldest son of Owen, with a great following made assault,
in an evil hour for himself, on the castle of Usk, which
had been put into some condition for defence, and wherein
at that time were the lord Grey, of Codnor, sir John
Greyndour [2], and many other soldiers of the king. For
those same lords, sallying forth manfully, took him captive,
and pursuing his men even to the hill-country of Higher
Gwent, through the river Usk, there slew with fire and
the edge of the sword many of them, and above all
the abbot of Llanthony, and they crushed them without
ceasing, driving them through the monks' wood, where
the said Griffith was taken [3]. And their captives, to
the number of three hundred, they beheaded in front
of the same castle near Ponfald; and certain prisoners of
more noble birth they brought, along with the same
Griffith, to the king. The which Griffith, being held in
captivity for six years, at last in the Tower of London was

---

[1] Lionel, duke of Clarence, married, as his second wife, Violante
Visconti, daughter of Gian Galeazzo, duke of Milan, on the 28th May,
1368, and died in the following October.

[2] Richard de Grey, baron Grey of Codnor, and sir John Greyndour,
or Grendor.

[3] This defeat of Glendower's followers took place at " Pwl-Melyn
mountain near Usk." Owen's brother Tudor was slain. It followed
immediately on the defeat at Grosmont of 11th March, 1405. Adam's
date is a little too early: perhaps he has confused the dates of
the two battles. The *Annales Henrici quarti*, 399, gives the date as
the 5th May. Otterbourne, 251, on the other hand, places the battle
as early as the 15th March. See Wylie, *Henry the Fourth*, ij. 171;
Kingsford, *Henry V.*, 52. Monkswood lies about a mile and a half
north-west of Usk.

cut off by a pestilence. And from that time forth in those A.D. 1405. parts the fortunes of Owen waned.

At length, setting out from Aiguebelle, I passed under A.D. 1406. a safe-conduct through Grande Chartreuse, and through the midst of Burgundy, Beaune, the nurse of the better wine of France, and Dijon, to Troyes in Champagne; and I crossed over the borders of the Isle of France to Provins and Brie-Comte-Robert, and to Paris; and at last I came down by way of Clermont and Amiens (where I saw the head of Saint John Baptist) and Arras, to Bruges in Flanders. And there Richard Lancaster, king of arms [1], counselled me, for that the king threatened me with death, that I should in no wise enter into England, without his royal grace first assured; which indeed he promised to obtain for me, and on account of which I waited for him in A.D. 1406<br>-1408. those parts for the space of two years, although to no purpose.

I had it also that all my benefices had been granted to others, [whereby my substance] was forspent to the sum of hundreds of marks. To be brief, I pondered many things. But with Job I cried: "Shall we receive good at the hand of God, and shall we not receive evil?" [2]

In the said space of two years I travelled through the lands of Flanders and France and Normandy and Brittany, serving as counsel to many bishops and abbots and princes; and I got me some gain thereby. And twice in that season, while I was sleeping, I was clean stripped, at least on the second time, even to my breeches, by certain Welshmen in whom I had placed my trust. And assuredly on that same day I afterwards had of the bounty of the aforesaid princes one hundred and twenty crowns.

The earl of Northumberland and the lord of Bardolf [3], after many misfortunes, first fleeing from before the face of

---

[1] Richard del Brugg, or Brugge, created Lancaster king of arms by Henry IV.　　　　　　　　　　　　[2] Job ij. 10.

[3] Thomas Bardolf, baron Bardolf of Wormegay.

A.D. 1406
-1408. king Henry into Scotland, (the son of the lord Henry Percy, and grandson and heir of the same earl, having been surrendered as hostage,) thence passed under a safe-conduct into Wales to Owen, seeking aid, and there they tarried for a season; and at length they were overthrown in stricken field by the English under my lord of Powis[1]. Then they came into France also, under safe-conduct, seeking aid against the same king, but labouring in vain, for that the duke of Orleans withstood them. And, because I too often held converse with them, I thereby drew down on me the greater wrath of king Henry, when he knew thereof. At last the earl was traitorously enticed again into Scotland and thence into England by certain who promised under false seals that he should have the kingdom. And he held out to me great advancement, if I should pass over along with him; but God visited mine heart, and I bethought me: "Adam, thus beset in a maze, place thyself in the hand of the Lord!" And God sent an evil spirit, and according to their deserts, between the king and the same earl, after the way of Abimelech, as it is read in the book of Judges [2]. And therefore I turned my cloak, and I inclined my footsteps to my lord of Powis, abiding the favour of the king and his kingdom, if God should grant it; and so it came to pass.

A.D. 1408. The aforesaid lords passed over into Scotland and thence with an armed band into England, trusting to have the kingdom for themselves. But the sheriff of York [3], being well ware of their coming, crushed them in battle and beheaded them, and sent their heads to king Henry; which were afterwards set up beyond London bridge [4]. And when

---

[1] Edward de Cherleton, baron Cherleton, feudal lord of Powis, K.G.
[2] ix. 23.     [3] Thomas Rokeby.
[4] They were defeated at Bramham Moor, 19th February, 1408. Bardolf died of his wounds. His body was quartered, and his head was set up over one of the gates of Lincoln. Northumberland fell on the field. His body was quartered and beheaded.

I heard these things, I, the writer of this history, gave
thanks unto Him who foreseeth what is to come, for that
I had stayed behind.

By the means and furtherance of the duke of Burgundy,
the duke of Orleans, on account of his unheard-of greed
passing all bounds, (the infirmity of the king of France
being the cause thereof,) although he was the king's
brother, was put to death as a usurper of the government[1]. Whence arose a mighty seething up of rebellion,
which even now has not ceased, within the realm of
France, as all men know. The bishop of Liége[2], who
was the brother of the wife of the duke of Burgundy,
came to Paris, to his aid, with five thousand armed men;
and this aid forthwith the same duke did afterwards reward
in full. For when the bishop's diocese rose in wide rebellion,
for that he would not be ordained to the priesthood, and
when by authority of the antipope another was chosen in
his stead, his adversary was slain in mortal battle by the
said duke, together with sixteen thousand men and upwards;
and the same bishop was restored unto his high estate.

In truth, there ought to be in France twelve peers, to
wit, three dukes and three counts, spiritual; and three
dukes and three counts, temporal; as appears in the
lines :—

> " Dukes temporal in France are three :
> First name we him of Burgundy;
> And peers of him are princes twain
> Of Normandy and Aquitaine.
>
> High prelates of the same degree
> And rank are also counted three;

---

[1] Louis, duke of Orleans, brother of Charles VI., was murdered by
John the Fearless, duke of Burgundy, his cousin, on the 23rd November,
1407.

[2] John of Bavaria, bishop of Liége, 1390–1417, son of Albert, count
of Holland. He died in 1428. His sister Margaret was duchess of
Burgundy.

Their sees are Rheims, a mighty one,
And Langres next, and eke Laon.

Great counts we number thrice again,
Of Toulouse, Flanders, and Champagne;
And bishops in the same array
Of Chalons, Noyon, and Beauvais."

But the king, treating the peerages with scorn, seized them to himself on every opportunity, so that he now has gotten to himself four of those which are temporal and has joined them to the crown; and other two, of Burgundy and Flanders to wit, the same duke holds. And this was the source of evils, because, when the king fell sick, the duke of Burgundy claimed that the governance of the realm belonged to him only.

The master of Prussia, of the order of chivalry of Saint Mary of the Teutons, in these days marched into the realm of the Turks, and conquered in battle their king, together with five hundred knights who were driven in flight. But straightway afterwards he himself, by reason of his too great pride, was defeated by the king of Poland[1].

From the Teutons I had it that, in honour of Arthur, king of Britain, for that he delivered them from the hands of the Romans, throughout all the cities and chief places of Germany great festivals are held in honour of stranger princes who come thither. The public place of the city, being endowed with revenues for the purpose, is decked out; and wines and spices, and dances with all melody of music, and with courteous welcome of lords and ladies, are lavished right nobly.

Master John Trevaur, doctor of laws and bishop of St. Asaph, casting off his special friendship for the English, threw in his lot with the fortunes of Owen, in peace and in war; and, having twice passed over into France seeking

---

[1] The Teutonic knights, under their master Ulrich von Jungingen, were disastrously defeated, in 1410, by Vladislas, king of Poland, at Tannenberg, near Potsdam.

aid of armed men, he was translated to a see among the   A.D. 1410.
Indians; and the abbot of Llanegwast [1] was chosen bishop
of St. Asaph in his stead. But the same master John, thus
fallen into ill fortune, betook himself to Rome, where, beyond Tiber, on the fifth day of October, in the year of our
Lord 1412, he died [2].

While I was in Bruges, the above-named earl of North-   A.D. 1406.
umberland and lord of Bardolf were lodged, the one in the
monastery of Eeckhout [3], and the other in a hospice in the
midst of the city. And on the eve of Saint Brice (12th
November), in the twilight of the evening, there came from
the side of England in the air a ball of fire, greater than
a large barrel, lighting up, as it were, the whole world.
And, as it drew near, all men were astounded and stood in
fear lest the city should be destroyed. But it passed on

---

[1] Or de Valle Crucis abbey, co. Denbigh.

[2] John Trevaur, or Trevor, created bishop of St. Asaph in 1395.
After serving the crown staunchly for many years, he went over to
Owen in 1404, and was immediately deprived. He was concerned in
Northumberland's rebellion, and fled with him into Scotland in 1405;
and he remained true to Owen's cause for the rest of his life (Wylie,
*Henry the Fourth*, ij. 10). The date of his death is uncertain. An
epitaph in the chapel of the infirmary of the abbey of St. Victor of
Paris is said to mark the place of his burial. But, according to
Browne Willis (Le Neve, *Fasti*, i. 70), the words of the inscription
are: "Johannes episcopus Hereford, in Wallia, qui obiit anno Domini
1410, die Veneris, 10° mensis Aprilis." This reading, however, is
differently given by Bradley, *Owen Glyndwr*, 299, who does not quote
his authority: "Johannes episcopus Asaphensis in Wallia, qui obiit
A.D. 1410, die secundo mensis Aprilis." The see was filled in 1411
by the appointment of Robert of Lancaster, who was probably the
abbot of Valle Crucis mentioned by Adam, for he seems to have been
connected with that house, an existing charter of his being dated
there (Le Neve, i. 71). Adam was no doubt personally acquainted
with Trevaur, and he is curiously precise in his statement of the place
and date of his death. But, whatever the rest of the statement may
be worth, the fact that the see was filled in 1411 and not till then
seems to substantiate the date of 1410 as the year of Trevaur's death;
and 1412 in the text may be only a clerical error.

[3] The monastery of St. Bartholomew of Eeckhout, an early foundation, which was demolished in 1798.

A.D. 1406. straight against the belfry of Saint Mary, and, being severed
in twain by the blow, it drove apart its two portions to
fall over against the doors of the said earl and lord: a
mighty token, as did afterwards appear, of their ruin.

In the chronicles of the same monastery, I found this
which here follows, written in mockery of the French,
for that in former days they were routed by the men of
Flanders :—

*The Passion of the French, according to the Flemings* [1].

Likewise I found it recorded in the chronicle of Martinus,
in the history of Constantine the second, that in a very
ancient tomb at Constantinople there was found a plate of
gold with this writing thereon: " Jesus Christ shall be
born of the Virgin Mary; and I believe in Him." Also,
that in Spain a certain Jew, while he was breaking up
some stony ground wherein to plant vines, found in
the middle of a rock which he clove asunder a book of
leaves of stone containing the same words, and furthermore setting forth the division of the course of the
world into three parts, from Adam even unto Antichrist,
and of each part its conditions. And of Christ it thus
began: "Jesus Christ, the Son of God, shall be born of
the Virgin Mary, and He shall suffer for the people; and
I believe in Him. And I shall be found in the days of

---

[1] The mock chronicle is so offensively profane that it is better left
without translation. The battle of Courtrai, in which the French
army under Robert of Artois was routed with fearful slaughter, was
fought on the 11th July, 1302.

Ferdinand, king of Castille." And thus it was. And the A.D. 1406.
Jew was baptized.

Out of the annals of the Hebrews, lo!, the tokens which
shall forerun the Day of Judgement: On the first day,
shall the sea rise forty cubits above all the mountains, not
outspread, but standing, after the fashion of a wall, in its
own place. On the second day, it shall fall again, so that
it shall scarce be seen. On the third day, all fishes shall
lift up a cry unto heaven, which God only doth understand; and I believe that they shall render the last witness
to the Creator. On the fourth day, the seas and all waters
shall burn with fire. On the fifth day, all trees and herbs
shall sweat a bloody dew; and all the fowls of the air, after
their kind, shall flock together, and shall taste naught
while they meditate on their Creator. On the sixth day,
buildings shall fall; and there shall be thunder-bolts of
fire from the setting of the sun even to his rising. On
the seventh day, rocks shall clash together and shall be
rent in four pieces, the sound whereof God alone knoweth.
On the eighth day, there shall be so mighty a quaking of
the earth, that all things on the face thereof shall be laid
low. On the ninth day, all things which are rough shall be
ground down to powder, and the earth shall be made plain.
On the tenth day, men shall come forth from the caves,
and for terror they shall not be able to speak together.
On the eleventh day, all bones of dead men shall be laid
bare above their sepulchres. On the twelfth day, the stars
and constellations and all the other bodies of the firmament
shall send forth perplexed and fiery rays; and the beasts
of the earth shall gather in the fields, with a mighty
lowing, tasting naught. On the thirteenth day, all living
beings shall die, and shall rise again with the dead. On
the fourteenth day, the heavens and the earth shall burn
with fire. On the fifteenth day, there shall be made a new
heaven and a new earth, and all men shall rise again to
receive judgement; and on that day may the Son of the

A.D. 1406. Virgin, who shall judge the world because He hath redeemed it with His blood, place us on His right hand in company with the sheep!

Yet, before those tokens come to pass, Antichrist shall strive to deceive the world for a season of four weeks. In the first week, he shall labour, by declaring that he is the Christ promised by the law, to pervert the meaning of Holy Writ, and to destroy the law of Christ and to stablish his own. And he shall sit in the temple, as it were God, that he may take away the law of Christ (Daniel xj. " They shall place the abomination that maketh desolate "[1]; with the gloss). In the second week, by the working of miracles; for he shall make fire come down from heaven on the earth [2] through an evil spirit, even as Christ through the Holy Ghost (Revelation xiij.; with the gloss). In the third week, by abundance of gifts, for the treasures of the earth shall be laid open unto him [3] by the devils, and he shall share them, together with the land, among his followers (Daniel xj.; with the gloss). In the fourth week, by the wreaking of torments, for those whom he shall not be able to entice in the things aforenamed he shall slay cruelly; as in Revelation, concerning Elias and Enoch and others who resist him.

Lo!, here are verses that tell forth the tokens of the Judgement :—

"Ere the Judgement draweth near,
    All the world perplexed shall be ;
Tokens rough and signs of fear
    Thrice five days shall mortals see.

Jerome, skilled in Hebrew lore,
    Warnings of these tokens sent,
That the wicked may implore
    Grace from lasting punishment.

---

[1] Dan. xj. 31.        [2] Rev. xiij. 13.        [3] Dan. xj. 43.

Witness they shall bear and prove,       1406.
   With the old world's passing knell,
Cruel torments, if we love
   Earthly blandishments too well.

Ocean first aloft shall pile
   All his waters in a heap,
Topping mountain peaks, the while
   Gathered up from out the deep.

Then to earth again he sinks;
   Eye of man shall scarce discern
Where within his bed he shrinks,
   Till his wonted state return.

Fishes from the flood shall rise,
   Heaven with lowings deep assail;
Flocking birds with doleful cries
   Loud shall mourn, and beasts shall wail.

Dawns the fourth and dreadful day:
   Flame devours the mighty deep;
Rivers burn; and in dismay,
   Parched with fear, men pale and weep.

Clouds shall veil the fifth day's sun;
   Blood shall growing herbs bedew,
Blood like sweat all earth o'errun,
   Blood the living trees embrue.

Shattered is the embattled wall,
   Tower and town uprooted lie;
Scarce in war might worse befall,
   For the hour of doom is nigh.

Rock with rock shall clash in fight;
   Men shall pray, in terror driven,
Cave and mountain if they might
   Hide them from the wrath of Heaven.

Lo!, the earth shall quake again;
  Creatures stumble all amazed;
Places rough shall now be plain,
  Hills abased and valleys raised.

They erstwhile who caverns sought
  Far afield are scatterèd,
Witless wanderers distraught,
  Stricken dumb with awful dread.

Ten days past! ten portents told!
  Lo!, from out the bursten tomb,
(Sight of horror to behold!)
  Dead men's skeletons do come.

Heaven upon the cowering world
  Presseth with a stifling force;
Stars from out their spheros are hurled;
  Flames through aëry spaces course.

All who here below remain
  Living on the earth shall die,
With the dead to rise again
  And be judgèd righteously.

Seventh twice-told the day doth rise,
  Red with purifying flame,
With its blast doth melt the skies
  And the earth's dissolving frame.

Signs and wonders now are past;
  Heaven and earth anew God makes.
Hark!, the angel's trumpet-blast
  From their sleep the dead awakes."

"From Heaven above descending, see
  The Lord in clouds of majesty,
To judge mankind, the quick, the dead,
  In Josaphat's vale gatherèd.

For doom shall every life be told;
The wicked shall the Cross behold,
The Crown, the Lance, and Him beside,
The One they pierced and crucified.

No heart may then its secret veil,
Nor wealth nor power in aught avail;
God's treasure shall the just possess,
And worldlings wail their wickedness.

What tongue may tell of heavenly bliss?
What tongue, the pain of hell's abyss?
For saints God's fount of honour flows;
The damned are whelmed in endless woes.

So may each man with tears repent
And pray for God's enlightenment,
Regardful of the Judge to be,
And in the evil day go free!

No words the sinner's faults condone
Before that stern and righteous throne;
Nor plea nor patron there may rise,
To aid us in the great assize.

Distinction then there shall not be
Of clergy and of laity;
No favour may that Just One show,
Who seeketh out the truth to know.

There none may allegation try,
Exception take, nor join reply;
Appeal to Holy See is vain;
The sentence none may turn again.

No fee for bull or scribe, or for
Pope's chamberlain or janitor;
The wicked He delivereth
To torment's ever-living death.

A dread to all, I rise and speak :
Ye clergy, hearken, proud or meek ;
Secure, I fear not ; lo !, my word
Shall smite you like keen-tempered sword.

To prelate and to cardinal,
To monk and nun shall woe befall,
To grudging priest, and clerk whose greed
Doth sell his soul for earthly meed.

The more their gain, more meagre they,
Like men to dropsy fall'n a prey,
Who drink and yet more thirsty grow ;
For rest may misers never know.

The unjust judge the right perverts,
And breaks the laws himself asserts,
Of vengeance unaware ; for he,
Condemner, shall condemnèd be.

Man dies and moulders in the earth ;
His avarice, what is it worth,
Vain, empty tumult of the mind ?
The fool must leave his wealth behind.

His body in vile shroud lies lorn,
His soul to place of torment borne,
Where, writhing like wind-shaken reed,
For ransom it may never plead.

Ye judges, ponder what ye are !
What may you to the Lord declare ?
Shall Codex or Digest suffice ?
For Christ judge, plaintiff, witness is.

Ye clerks, who softly feed and lie
On beds of down and tapestry ;
Beware, who now your pleasure take,
Confession grievous ye must make.

Ye richly feast, and bid the door
Be shut against the hungry poor;
They beg a dole in humble wise,
Yet naught ye give, save blasphemies.

Your flesh with flesh ye stuff and fill,
And hoarded wealth ye spend and spill;
Rare wines from goblets large ye drain,
And stretch your maw for food again.

'In works of pity,' saith the Lord,
'All ye who wrought have gained reward;
'Who cared not for my poor, depart!
'But ye who cared, be glad of heart!'

Now all is done. The damnèd lie
Rejected, ground in agony;
But honoured, comforted, the blest
Are called to their eternal rest."

The aforesaid Lancaster king of arms, returning back
from England, made known to me, the writer of this
history, at Paris, that he had spoken with the king to
make my peace, but that both by reason of my commerce
with the said earl of Northumberland and of disparage-
ments written of me by my rivals from Rome, there was
no means of reconciliation with him, for that his indignation waxed stronger day by day. Wherefore, I, Adam, the
writer of this history, made a declaration before the same
king of arms that I would feign myself Owen's man, and
with my following would cross over into Wales unto him;
and thence, taking my chance, I would steal away from
him to my lord of Powis, to await under his care the king's
favour. And so it came to pass. And this declaration
saved me my life. Snares were laid for me by sea; and
eight ships of Devon chased me for two livelong days, and
again and again I was hunted like a hare by so many
hounds.

But at last, through the prayers of Saint Thomas of

A.D. 1408. India, whom I beheld in a vision praying to God that he would bless me, I escaped to the port of St. Pol de Leon in Brittany ; and there in the chapel of Saint Theliau, where too he slew a dragon one hundred and twenty feet in length, committing myself to his care, I daily celebrated mass.

A.D. 1408 –1411. At length, taking my chance, I landed in Wales at the port of Barmouth[1], and there I hid in the hills and caves and thickets, before that I could come unto my said lord of Powis, because at that time he had taken to wife, in the parts of Devon, the daughter of the earl of the same[2] ; sorely tormented with many and great perils of death and capture and false brethren, and of hunger and thirst, and passing many nights without sleep for fear of the attacks of foes. Moreover, on behalf of the same Owen, when it was found out that I had sent to my said lord for a safe-conduct, I was laid under the close restraint of pledges. But at last, when my lord had come again to his own country, and when I had gotten from him letters of leave to come unto him and to rest safe with him, I gat me by night and in secret unto him at his castle of Pool ; and there and in the parish church of the same, not daring to pass outside his domain, like a poor chaplain only getting victuals for saying mass, shunned by thankless kin and those who were once my friends, I led a life sorry enough —and how sorry God in His heart doth know.

A.D. 1411. Meantime, while I there abode, among the other gentlemen of Owen's party, three men of fame, to wit Philip Scudamore of Troy, Rhys ap Griffith of Cardigan, and Rhys ap Tudor of Anglesey, being taken by the captain of the same castle, were drawn to the gallows and hanged ; the first at Shrewsbury, whose head is still there set up beyond bridge, the second at London, and the third at Chester.

---

[1] The native name is Abermaw, the "Abermo" of the MS.

[2] Powis's second wife ; not a daughter of the earl of Devon, but Elizabeth, daughter of sir John Berkeley, of Beverstone, co. Gloucester.

At length, at the instance of my said lord, and of David A.D. 1411.
Holbache, a man of high estate, I had the king's grace by
his letters [1]; which too I got proclaimed at Shrewsbury.
And then I passed over thither on foot, to visit mine old
friends; and I had of them horses twain and one hundred
shillings to my joy; and I hired me a servant; and, like
to one new-born, I began somewhat to fashion again my
condition as before mine exile. Then I gat me to mine own
country, among old friends and kinsmen, whom I had
advanced and had otherwise raised up in no small degree,
and among my debtors, hoping myself to be comforted;
but I found them to be not only thankless, and hurling
reproaches to boot, but, for fear I should exact of them
anything of mine own, even seekers after my ruin. As
the proverb runs: not for myself but for what I had they
loved me, and so, when fortune fled, they deserted me. And
as the poet says: I begged a loan of my friend, and lost
friend and money too.

Thence into England, with trembling heart but with
a cheerful countenance, I passed, to visit my lords and
ancient friends; and I took count of benefices and goods
lost beyond recall. In parliament was I, along with other
doctors; and little by little, with the help of God, I
enlarged mine heart and my countenance and my spirit.

By my lord of Canterbury I was restored in his court at
Canterbury, and I was preferred to the good church of
Merstham; and, like another Job, I gathered to myself
servants, and books, and garments, and household goods,
wherefore blessed be God for ever and ever!

The wife of Owen [2], together with his two daughters [3] A.D. 1409.

---

[1] A pardon was issued to Adam on the 20th March, 1411 (Patent
Roll, 12 Hen. IV., m. 18). David Holbache (the MS. calls him Harlech), through whom it was obtained, sat in parliament for Shrewsbury, and founded Oswestry Grammar School.—Wylie, *Henry the
Fourth*, ij. 413; iij. 268.

[2] Margaret, daughter of sir David Hanmer.

[3] One of them was Mortimer's wife.

A.D. 1409.  and three granddaughters, daughters of sir Edmund Mortimer[1], and all household goods, was taken captive, and sent to London unto the king; and Owen, with his only remaining son Meredith, miserably lay in hiding in the open country, and in caves, and in the thickets of the mountains. To make all safe, and to curb fresh rebellions by means of the king's soldiers and at his costs, the glades and passes of Snowdon and of other mountains and forests of North Wales were held guarded.

A.D. 1413.  Henry the fourth, after that he had reigned with power for fourteen years, crushing those who rebelled against him, fell sick, having been poisoned; from which cause he had been tormented for five years by a rotting of the flesh, by a drying up of the eyes, and by a rupture of the intestines; and at Westminster, in the abbot's chamber, within the sanctuary, thereby fulfilling his horoscope that he should die in the Holy Land, in the year of our Lord 1412–13, and on the twentieth day of the month of March, he brought his days to a close. And he was carried away by water, and was buried at Canterbury[2]. That same rotting did the anointing at his coronation portend; for there ensued such a growth of lice, especially on his head, that he neither grew hair, nor could he have his head uncovered for many months. One of the nobles, at the time of his making the offering in the coronation-mass, fell from his hand to the ground; which then I with others standing by sought for diligently, and, when found, it was offered by him.

Henry the fifth, his first-born son by the daughter of the earl of Hereford, a youth upright and filled with virtues and wisdom, on the fourteenth day after his father's death,

---

[1] Mortimer's son, Lionel, was also taken. Owen's family fell into the hands of the English at the capture of Harlech, before February, 1409.—Wylie, *Henry the Fourth*, iij. 266.

[2] The body was conveyed by water to Faversham, and thence to Canterbury.

Passion Sunday, to wit, then falling (9th April), was A.D. 1413. crowned with great solemnity at Westminster.

On the same day an exceeding fierce and unwonted storm fell upon the hill-country of the realm, and smothered men and beasts and homesteads, and drowned out the valleys and the marshes in marvellous wise, with losses and perils to men beyond measure.

The new king made proclamation at the coronation-feast of pardon to all offenders, even to those guilty of high treason, provided that they should get them royal letters thereto prepared this side the festival of Saint John Baptist; whence, for those same letters he got large sums of money. And also in his parliament, then forthwith holden at Westminster [1], he levied on the clergy a tenth and on the laity a fifteenth. Also, in granting confirmations of the yearly stipends of certain persons, he reserved to himself the profits of the first year. Whatsoever fees too are wont to be levied when new reigns begin, he doubled. And against the Welsh and the Irish he sent forth an edict, that each man should get him to his own country; and thereby from them, for leave to remain, he gathered to himself much treasure [2].

In these days, by virtue of a certain exemption of pope A.D. 1411. Boniface the ninth, the university of Oxford with one accord and with a strong hand withstood the visitation of the metropolitan [3]; whence arose grievous strifes, and slaughter of men on both sides, because the gentry of the

---

[1] On the 15th May.

[2] Henry agreed to enforce the statute of the last reign for the expulsion of aliens, saving his prerogative of granting dispensations.

[3] This was in the year 1411. Adam has made the worst of things. Nobody was killed. The archbishop appealed to the king, who summoned the chancellor and the proctors to London and required them to resign. Ultimately, however, on the mediation of the prince of Wales, they were allowed to retain their offices. The bull of pope Boniface was revoked by John XXIII in November, 1411; the university submitted; and the archbishop's right of visitation was solemnly asserted in parliament.—Rashdall, *The Universities of Europe in the Middle Ages*, ij. 434.

A.D. 1411.  country came upon them to the succour of the said lord archbishop of Canterbury.  But the same lord at that time withdrew, doing naught; but he got such exemption revoked by pope John the twenty-third, and constrained the university to renounce it.

A.D. 1414.  Solemn envoys from France on behalf of the king's marriage and the peace of the two realms bided with him at their own costs for the space of two months, and at length, when they departed, he sent back with them his own envoys[1].

There were given to my lord the earl of March, and by him to my lord the king, two children, who were born in Wales, the male being of nine years and the female of seven years only, together with their common offspring which was being suckled by the mother, a great and unheard-of cause of wonder.

A.D. 1413.  Led by sir John Oldcastle, knight, who in right of his wife was styled lord of Cobham, the Lollards by their noisome doctrine, and in special by that touching the sacrament of the altar, troubled the church and her faithful sons and the realm.  They waxing stronger day by day in gathering multitudes, forbearance was withdrawn from them in certain places, with difficulty and under threat of interdict.  The said sir John was condemned a heretic[2] by the same lord of Canterbury and others his suffragans him assisting, and was delivered over by him a prisoner in the Tower of London.  Escaping thence[3] by night beyond the walls, and drawing unto him his followers by letters and by messengers, he secretly stirred the realm.

A.D. 1414.  On the eve of the Epiphany (5th January[4]), in order that he might attack and destroy the king, the brave champion

---

[1] The negotiations with the duke of Burgundy are here referred to. His envoys were in England from the 19th April to the 17th June, 1414.  Henry appointed ambassadors to treat on the 31st May.

[2] On the 10th October, 1413.

[3] On the 19th October.

[4] This date is too early; the gathering was planned for the night of the 9th–10th of the month.

of the faith who was filled with most Christian zeal, and all prelates and churches, he appointed the field called Fykettysfeld[1] for a gathering-place by night for him and his wicked confederates. But the field being occupied on that night with armed men by the king, who had cognizance thereof, they were taken captive in great numbers when they came thither, and were drawn, hanged, and burnt[2]. And among them sir Roger Acton, a knight of Shropshire, still for the space of a month was swinging on the gibbet[3]. Many who were condemned or were to be condemned were held prisoners in the Tower of London and elsewhere through the realm. This knight, the son of a tiler, sprung from a lowly family of Shropshire, being enriched with the plunder and spoils of the Welsh war, and being puffed up beyond measure, got himself honoured with the privilege of the military order and with the belt of knighthood by king Henry the fourth, and invested with the golden spurs by the king's two sons, the first-born who is now king, and the second-born now duke of Clarence. Yet afterwards, he blushed not to lift up his heel against them, thankless as he was.

On the nineteenth day of the month of February, in the year of our Lord 1413–14, my most illustrious lord, kinsman of our lord the king and of his brothers, as also of the earls of March, Arundel, Nottingham, and Stafford, as well as of Bergavenny and Spencer, and son of the earl of Arundel, deceased, the lord Thomas of Arundel, archbishop of Canterbury, primate of all England and legate of the see apostolic—the virtue, the lamp, the wisdom of the people, the torch and delight of the clergy, and staunch pillar of the church of the Christian faith, who gave me the good

[1] Or Little Lincoln's Fields.

[2] Sixty-nine were condemned; of whom thirty-seven were hanged, and of these seven were also burnt.—Ramsay, *Lancaster and York*, i. 180.

[3] He was executed on the 12th February.

A.D. 1414. churches of Kempsing in Kent and Merstham in Surrey, together with the prebend of Llandogo in Wales, and through whom I was hoping for promotion to greater things, even as he had promised,—suffering a sudden change [1] by the fate whereby all things sink to their setting, brought his days to an end, alas !, long time before I would have wished it, receiving with the joy of everlasting life that word of sweetness of the King of Heaven : "Good and faithful servant, enter thou into the joy of thy Lord." [2] And this ending of his life I beheld in a vision on that same night in London, in this wise : It seemed that he, leaving all his household and clad in short garments, as though about to journey afar, was running with great speed alone ; and when I strove with utmost toil to follow him, he handed to me a waxen candle, saying : "Cut this in twain betwixt us two" ; and so he vanished from my sight.    And awaking I understood that henceforth we were divided, and for his soul in all sorrow I said a mass ; and afterwards I was certified of his death.    He, at the time of his decease, was celebrating, with all the clergy of his province, none being excused for any reason or spared if able to work, a most solemn convocation, in the church of St. Paul, on behalf of the faith in which we stand [3]. Wherein, being a most powerful champion, he passed many good ordinances against the Lollards and heretics ; and among others, with consent of the king, this one : that any one guilty of heresy should lose his goods, both moveable and immoveable, and also on this account should be convicted of high treason, so that, besides the punishment of fire which is the penalty of heresy, he should be further punished by being drawn and hanged on the gibbet.

---

[1] He died unexpectedly of some affection of the throat.

[2] Matt. xxv. 21.

[3] Wake (*State of the Church and Clergy of England*, 350) mentions a convocation held 20th November, and an ecclesiastical council against the Lollards.

Further, that inquisitions and enquiries on this behalf should be holden throughout the shires by the king's justices [1]. These ordinances he got well brought into action before his death. The same convocation was resumed at Oxford, the very hatching-place of heresy ; and, while it was still being holden, he died, as told above.

Brother John Burghill, a covetous man, of the order of preachers, bishop of Lichfield [2], to his scandalous report throughout the realm, hid away a great sum of gold in a hole in his chamber ; and, by reason that the hole was open at the other end, a pair of jackdaws, (birds which are rightly called *monedulœ* from *moneta*,) which were minded to build their nest therein, cleared out the hole and scattered the gold among the trees and over the garden, to the profit of many. And this story I heard to my delight one day told at the table of my said lord by certain guests, great men of the realm.

To the see of Canterbury was translated master Henry Chicheley, doctor of laws, then bishop of St. Davids [3] ; in whose place was chosen master John Catterick to be bishop of St. Davids. To the same lord of Canterbury, when I departed from Oxford, I surrendered my civil chair. At length, within half a year thenceforth, he [master John Catterick] was chosen in succession to the said brother John Burghill departing this life, and in his place Stephen de Patryngton, of the order of Carmelites, was elected to the see of St. Davids [4].

The king held a parliament at Leicester [5] ; wherein were

---

[1] Adam is here anticipating. The statute against Lollardry which he quotes was passed in the parliament of Leicester, after Arundel's death. But the archbishop no doubt had a hand in preparing the enactment.

[2] Translated from Llandaff to Lichfield, 1398. Died 20th May, 1414.

[3] Translated to Canterbury, 27th April, 1414.

[4] Catterick was translated from St. Davids to Lichfield, 1st February, 1415.

[5] From 30th April to 29th May, 1414.

laid to the charge of prelates and clergy many transgressions and extortions and shortcomings in appropriations of wills, in misuse of hospitals and in regard of residence of curates, and in other things. The redress of these offences did the king give over to the convocation of the clergy; which being holden under the said archbishop of Canterbury in the church of St. Paul in London, there was in many things redress ordained, especially in regard of wills, to wit: that under one hundred shillings value twelvepence be paid, and so up to twenty pounds; and beyond that sum, up to one hundred pounds, ten shillings; and so, up to one thousand pounds, for every hundred pounds, ten shillings; provided that, in whatever sum the value of the will should stand, the ordinary should not receive more than twenty pounds for all his pains. In this convocation were granted by the clergy, two tenths (although against custom, for the laity were wont to make grants first), before the grant of a fifteenth of temporal goods.

Now, at the cost of the clergy, to attend the general council of Constance, which was to be holden at the cost of the realm and especially at the cost of the clergy, for the redress of the said excesses and of the union of Christendom, were sent as solemn envoys the bishops of Bath and of Salisbury and of St. Davids, and the abbot of Westminster and the prior of Worcester, and the earl of Warwick, the lords Fitz-Hugh and Zouche, and also the knights sir Walter Hungerford and sir Ralph Rocheford[1].

---

[1] The envoys were Nicholas Bubbewith, bishop of Bath and Wells, Robert Hallum, bishop of Salisbury, John Catterick, bishop of St. Davids, Richard Beauchamp, earl of Warwick, William de Colchester, abbot of Westminster, Henry, baron Fitz-Hugh, John de Malvern, prior of Worcester, sir Walter Hungerford, and sir Ralph Rocheford. Their appointment was dated 20th October, 1414.—Rymer, *Fœdera*, ix. 167. William la Zouche, baron Zouche, of Harryngworth, was lieutenant of

In these days the Scots attacked the northern parts of England with no light hand.

The church of London, setting aside its own use which agreed not with others, took unto itself into daily use the offices of Salisbury, beginning on the first Sunday in Advent.

In this parliament [1], the king granted general pardon to all who should sue out letters to this end before the feast of Saint Michael [2]. It was also decreed that chaplains having stipends, if they held cures, should receive eight marks; otherwise seven marks only [3]. And, as otherwise on sacks of wool, now on bales of cloth a tribute was levied. On the eve of the Conception of the Blessed Virgin (7th December) the parliament was dissolved.

In this the second year of his reign, the king began to found near to Shene upon the bank of the Thames, three houses of religion, to wit one of the Carthusian order, the second of the order of Saint Bridget, and the third of the order of Saint Celestine, endowing them out of the possessions of the monks of France. The priories of Goldcliff and of Neath, otherwise French houses, are now in poverty [4].

The king sent far and wide throughout his realm certain

Calais, and was one of the envoys to the duke of Burgundy, 14th July, 1413.

[1] The parliament of the 19th November.

[2] Perhaps Adam makes this statement (which appears to have no foundation) in connection with the number of private petitions in this parliament.

[3] "Le roi voet qe nulles chapeleins annuelers preignent desore en avaunt pluis pur lour entier salarie par l'an, c'est assavoir, pur ses table, vesture, et autres necessaries, forsque vij. marcz, ne les chapeleins parochiels, qi sont retenuz a servir cures, ne preignent pur lour entier salarie annuell, c'est assavoir, pur ses choses avaunt ditz, sinon viij. marcz."—*Rot. Parl.* iv. 52.

[4] Henry V. founded the house of Jesus of Bethlehem at West Shene (Richmond) for Carthusians; and the house of Mount Sion, or Sion House, at Twickenham, of the order of Saint Bridget. The third foundation, to which Adam refers, may be the hermitage which was

A.D. 1414. trusty men in his service to visit each man of substance and to borrow money for him.

The king, in order to demand of the king of France the lands of his birthright which lay in that kingdom, as also his daughter in marriage for the maintenance of peace, sent forth solemn envoys into France, to wit, the bishops of Durham and of Norwich, and the earl of Dorset and the lord Scrope[1]. But they came back thence into England, as it were a laughing-stock, and without accomplishing aught. Wherefore the king and the great men of the realm, being wroth, turned the arms of their indignation against the French, as appears hereafter.

A.D. 1415. Monstrous perjury! Our pope John the twenty-third, false to his promises of union, other two, to wit Gregory and Benedict, being popes along with him (an unnatural thing), for that he was rebellious, and was otherwise guilty of perjuries, and murders, and adulteries, and simonies, and heresy, and other excesses, and for that he twice fled in secret and cowardly in vile raiment by way of disguise, by the said council was delivered to perpetual imprisonment[2].

On the sixteenth day of the month of June[3], in the

within the monastery of Shene (*Monasticon Anglic.*, vj. 29). Walsingham mentions the three foundations (ij. 300). Goldcliff was an alien Benedictine priory in Monmouthshire, given by Robert de Chandos, in 1113, to the abbey of Bec, in Normandy. The abbey of Neath in Glamorganshire was given to the Cistercians of Savigny, near Lyons, by Richard de Grainville and Constance, his wife, *temp.* Henry I.

[1] The envoys were Thomas Langley, bishop of Durham, Richard Courtenay, bishop of Norwich, Thomas Beaufort, earl of Dorset, and Richard de Grey, baron Grey of Codnor; 5th December, 1414.—Rymer, *Fœd.* ix. 183. Scrope was employed elsewhere.

[2] The pope succeeded in escaping from Constance on the 20th March, 1415, disguised as a groom, and evaded his pursuers for some time. He was deposed by the council of Constance on the 29th May. He was delivered into the care of duke Louis of Bavaria, who kept him in easy confinement at Heidelberg and Mannheim, and finally set him at liberty for a ransom. He died cardinal of Frascati, 1419.

[3] Henry left London on the 18th June, for Southampton.

third year of his reign, king Henry the fifth, after that he had first visited holy places with all devotion, set forth from London, in glorious chivalry, towards France, to subdue it in war, passing on his way to the sea-coast at Portsmouth. And there the envoys of the king of France coming to him and pretending to sue for peace [1] bought for a great sum of gold, from certain his councillors, to wit, Richard, earl of Cambridge, the brother of the duke of York, and also the lords Scrope and Grey [2], consent to his death, or at least a hindrance of his voyage. But they, being discovered by the earl of March, deservedly found a death worthy of such treason. And there came solemn envoys from the king of Aragon offering his daughter to wife to our king; in company with whom he sent over his own envoys thence [3].

Then making fair sail [4] he ploughed through the sea, and on the thirteenth day of August he landed on the coast of Normandy, near to Harfleur, with his host, according to his desire. And pitching his camp he attacked the place, and he tormented its area with underground mines, and shook the city and the walls with his engines and cannons; and in the end he won the surrender, along with the inhabitants all stripped and having cords and halters about their necks, and all the goods of the place. And presently he drove out the native inhabitants and placed therein his own Englishmen; and he chose the earl of Dorset to be captain [5]. Many perished in the siege by a flux of the

---

[1] The archbishop of Bourges and the bishop of Lisieux, who met Henry at Winchester on the 30th June, and departed on the 6th July.

[2] Richard Plantagenet, of Conisburgh, created earl of Cambridge, 1st May, 1414; Henry, baron Scrope, of Masham; and sir Thomas Grey, of Heton. Grey was executed forthwith; Cambridge and Scrope, after condemnation by their peers, on the 5th August.

[3] Commissions were issued to John Waterton and John Kemp to treat for the alliance and marriage, 25th July.—*Fœd.* ix. 293-4.

[4] On Sunday, the 11th August.

[5] Harfleur surrendered on the 22nd September. "The inhabitants

A.D. 1415. bowels, among whom were the bishop of Norwich, and the earls of Arundel and Suffolk[1]. Likewise thousands departed to their homes; some honourably, because they had leave; some discharged, because they were sick; and some with disgrace, because they deserted the field, to the indignation of the king[2].

The king, committing himself to God and to the fortune of the sword, brave and like a very lion, with scarce ten thousand warriors at his back[3], with caution led the march through the open country, yea, through the midst of France, for the bridges were broken down, towards Calais, to abide there. And against him came his adversaries of France, to the number of sixty thousand of the nobles and men of rank[4], nigh Agincourt in Picardy. Battle was joined, and, blessed be God!, the victory fell to our king, on whose side only seven and twenty were slain, among whom the men of noble birth who died were the duke of York, and the young earl of Suffolk, sir [Richard] Kyghley and sir [John]

were taken under the king's protection, and divided into three classes: (1) those who were good for ransom; (2) the able-bodied, who might be allowed to stay on taking an oath of allegiance; (3) the weak and infirm, who would be out of place in a frontier stronghold. The last were forthwith marched out under escort, with just as much as they could carry in their hands; and so turned over to the care of their countrymen at Lillebonne (24th September)."—Ramsay, *Lancaster and York*, i. 204. Dorset was left with a garrison of 300 lances and 900 bows.—*Ibid.* 205.

[1] Richard Courtenay, bishop of Norwich, died on the 15th September; Michael de la Pole, earl of Suffolk, also died during the siege, 18th September; Thomas Fitzalan, earl of Arundel, after the surrender, on the 13th October.

[2] The losses by sickness and desertion are estimated to have been about one-third of the whole force.

[3] Henry marched from Harfleur on the 8th or 9th October. The number of the English who fought at Agincourt has been placed at 900 to 1,000 men-at-arms, and 3,000, or, according to some writers, 5,000, archers.—*Lanc. and York*, i. 205.

[4] The French were perhaps about four times as numerous as the English.

Skidmore, knights, and David Gam, of Breconshire[1].  On the side of the French, who were slain or captured or put to flight, and who brought with them their treasure and, although to their own confusion, the king's baggage train, the dukes of Orleans and Bourbon and six counts were made prisoners; and three dukes, six counts, three and twenty barons, ninety lords, and fourteen hundred gentlemen who bore coat armour, and seven thousand of the commons fell on the field[2].

On the fourth day of November, under my lord John, duke of Bedford, the king's second brother, and in his absence his lieutenant, began at London a solemn parliament[3], to provide supplies to the king both of men and money; wherein it was agreed by the commons that the full fifteenth, which had been granted, as above, to be paid at the feast of the Purification of the Blessed Virgin next coming (2nd February), should be levied forthwith to the king's use before the feast of Saint Lucy the virgin (13th December).  There was likewise granted another fifteenth for the year next following, to be paid on the feast of Saint Martin (11th November).  To the king also, for the term of his life: as to merchandise on wool-sacks four marks, and on wine-tuns three shillings, and on other goods, each and every, poundage of twelvepence; and rightly, for it was in honour of his deeds of valour.

In the king's praise it was thus that a certain versemaker wrote:—

[1] Edward, son of Edmund of Langley, succeeded his father as duke of York in 1402.  Michael de la Pole, earl of Suffolk, had just succeeded his father, Michael, who had died before Harfleur.  The name of sir John Skidmore does not appear in other lists of the slain.  The number varies in the works of English contemporary writers, the highest estimate being about one hundred.  French writers raise the number to 1,600.—Nicolas, *Hist. Batt. Agincourt*, 135.

[2] Perhaps these figures may be fairly correct.  The chroniclers generally make them range from 3,000 or 4,000 to 11,000 or 12,000.

[3] It sat from the 4th to the 12th November.

"Now, all ye toiling English, rest and pray;
Fair fell the victory on Crispin's day,
When France's envious power sank prone to earth:
France, who derided England's native worth.
O hateful foe, that scornèd worth was vowed
To humble thee; it planted courage proud
In our king's heart; in thine was slothfulness.
This gift is Heaven's; Christ's name we praise and
    bless.
Thrust back is guile; gone, superstitious craft;
Minds sullen sink, drenched with a bitter draught."

On the feast of Saint Brice (13th November) the parliament was dissolved.

On the nineteenth day of the month of November next following, in the church of St. Paul, in London, under master Henry Chicheley, archbishop of Canterbury, a convocation of the clergy was holden in aid of the king's needs, for that he was deprived of his substance by the enemy. Wherein, notwithstanding that a whole tenth remained to be levied on the feast of the Purification (2nd February) next coming, as aforetold, other two tenths were granted to the king to be levied, at the two next feasts of Saint Martin in the winter (11th November), on benefices not yet taxed, which should reach to the annual value of ten pounds and upwards, the same to be valued by the ordinary. But from this grant the importunity of the writer of this history got relief for the benefices of Wales, as being impoverished by war. To the envoys likewise of the clergy, then present at the general council at Constance on behalf of the union of the church, there was granted an aid for their costs.

Saint George's day (23rd April), at the instance of the king, was prolonged into a double festival for a holiday from toil.

On the twenty-third day of the month of November, in

the year of our Lord 1415, the king coming from Calais to
London, bringing his captives, was met one mile without
the city by the clergy in procession, and at four miles, in
the place called Blackheath, by the noblemen and citizens
on horseback, to the number of ten thousand, clad in red,
with hoods party black and white, exulting in heart.
At the entrance of London bridge was an armed giant,
like to a second Pallas, outtopping the walls in height,
having a spear even like to the spear of Turnus (whereby
the same Pallas perished, pierced through full four feet and
a half : concerning whom see above [1], book vj., chapter xxj.
at the end) and a mighty axe, by the very wind of which
not only might woods be laid low, but even an army
might be slain ; and by his side was his wife, so huge that
not only was she fit in truth to give birth to giant devils,
but even to bring forth towers of hell—and they were set
beyond the gate, as warders thereof, together with the
king's arms.  In the midst of the bridge, in front of the
drawbridge, were two outworks, in one of which on the
right hand was a lion bearing a lance, and in the other an
antelope having a shield of the arms of the king hung
about his neck, and beyond the bridge was a figure of
Saint George armed becomingly—and these were placed to
guard the bridge.  Conduits, richly decked and running
with wine, gave good cheer to all who would drink.  At
the cross in the midst of Cheap, from one side to the other,
abutting on the church of St. Peter [2], was placed a triple
building, rising in steps, with a wonderful show of battlements and with turrets and bulwarks, and set about with
shields of arms of the realm and of the princes thereof ;

[1] Adam refers to Higden's " Polychronicon," to which his chronicle
was added as a supplement. The passage is as follows : " Hujus etiam
imperatoris [Henrici] diebus repertum est Romæ illud incorruptum
Pallantis corpus, cum hiatu vulneris quatuor pedum et semis. Corpus
ejus altitudinem muri vincebat."—*Polychron.* (Rolls series), vij. 148.

[2] The parish church of St. Peter the Apostle, or St. Peter in Cheap,
which stood by the cross, at the corner of Wood Street.

A.D. 1415.  and it was made up of planks by the cunning of carpenters
and painters, and draped with stout canvas painted in the
resemblance of walls of varied porphyry and marble and
ivory, whereon. was written, "Glorious things are spoken
of thee, O city of God"[1]; and it was filled in suitable wise
with angels and with singers and with instruments of
music. And from its iron gates there issued forth six
stately citizens, bearing two golden bowls filled with gold,
which were offered unto the king. And after the manner
of those who welcomed king David when he had slain
Goliath, there met the king, hard by the lower conduit,
maidens dancing and singing, with choirs and drums and
golden viols. In a word: the city was decked in all the
raiment of gladness, and rightfully there was great joy
among the people[2].

The king, dismounting at St. Paul's, visited the holy
cross, and the tomb of Saint Erkenwald[3], and the high altar,
with much reverence and giving of alms; and thence he
departed towards Westminster, there to dine; and on the
morrow he caused a solemn funeral service, on behalf of

---

[1] Ps. lxxxvij. 3.

[2] Compare the account of the pageants given in the *Gesta Henrici
Quinti* (by the king's chaplain, now identified as Elmham), ed.
B. Williams (English Historical Society), 1850; and also that in
Elmham's "Liber Metricus" in *Memorials of Henry the Fifth* (Rolls
series), ed. C. A. Cole, 1858. The six stately citizens with their bowls
of gold, issuing from the gates of the castle in Cheap, do not appear
in the other accounts. Perhaps Adam has created them out of the
deputation from the city to make an offering to the king: "And on
the morwe after, it was Soneday and the xxiiij day of November, the
maire and alle the aldermen, with two hundred of the beste comoners
of London, wente to Westminster to the king and present hym with
a ml. pound in too basynes of gold worth v^c. li."—*Chronicle of
London* (ed. Nicolas), 1827, p. 103.

[3] "Monuments in this Church [St. Paul's] be these: First, as
I reade, of Erkenwalde, Bishop of London, buried in the old Church,
about the yeere of Christ, 700, whose body was translated into the new
work in the yeere 1140, being richly shrined above the Quire, behinde
the high Altar."—Stow, *Survey of London*, 1633, p. 358.

those who had fallen on either side in the war, to be A.D. 1415. celebrated by bishops and clergy at St. Paul's.

The aforetold capture of Harfleur and the victory of the battle of Agincourt are put shortly in this verse:—

> " Harfleur Maurice hath fordone ;
> Agincourt hath Crispin won." [1]

And the date of the year of our Lord 1415 is found in the same verse, thus: M. once, C. thrice, L. twice, V. twice, and I. five times, added together [2]. The festivals of the two saints brought with them those victories.

Died Owen Glendower, after that during four years he had lain hidden from the face of the king and the realm ; and in the night season he was buried by his followers. But his burial having been discovered by his adversaries, he was laid in the grave a second time ; and where his body was bestowed may no man know [3].

The king with great reverence went on foot in pilgrimage A.D. 1416. from Shrewsbury to St. Winifred's well in North Wales [4].

The earl of Dorset, captain of Harfleur, marching out with five hundred men, slew of the French who assaulted him to the number of two thousand, and took many captive [5].

---

[1] The verse occurs in Elmham's " Liber Metricus."

[2] He means that these letters occur in the line as many times as he has stated ; and that, by giving them their value as Roman numerals and adding them together, the result is 1415. This is also the meaning of the gloss in the " Liber Metricus," viz. "Annus Domini m.cccc.xv. per literas numerales."

[3] The exact date of Owen's death is uncertain. On the 5th July, 1415, sir Gilbert Talbot was commissioned to treat with him with a view to his submission ; and again, on the 24th February, 1416, to treat with Owen's son, Meredith, for the same purpose (*Fœdera*, ix. 283, 331). The latter commission, not being to treat with Owen direct, seems to imply uncertainty of where he was to be found. The traditional date of his death is the 20th September, 1415. See Wylie, *Henry the Fourth*, iij. 270.

[4] Holywell St. Winifred, co. Flint. This pilgrimage of Henry V. does not appear to be recorded elsewhere. If Adam is correct in his statement, it probably took place early in 1416.

[5] Dorset, being pressed for supplies, set out on a plundering raid,

On the third day of March[1] was holden a parliament at Westminster, and in the church of St. Paul a convocation, wherein by clergy and people were granted in aid to the king two tenths and two fifteenths[2].

Sigismund, king of Hungary and of the Romans, after that he had striven for a year long in the general council at Constance for the unity of the church, and had delivered to prison pope John the twenty-third, who ruled in Rome, on account of his falsehoods, and after that he had visited the kings of Castille and of all Spain on behalf of the same unity, came through the realm of France into England for the stablishing of peace between those two kingdoms[3]. But, after that he had abode in London at the great cost of the realm, the business being thwarted by the cunning of the French, he returned again to the council of Constance.

A dreadful battle at sea was fought under the duke of Bedford, the king's brother, against the French, of whom many were brought captive with their ships into England, but their store of victuals was sent into Harfleur[4].

The king of the Romans aforesaid, departing from England, with his own hands sent forth scrolls, to be scattered abroad in the public places, whereof the wording was on this wise :—

"O happy England!, fare thee well, and be
Rejoiced and blest in glorious victory!

but was intercepted by the French, and only fought his way back to Harfleur with difficulty; 11th-13th March, 1416.

[1] Parliament met on the 16th March.

[2] It was only an acceleration of the tenth and fifteenth, granted in the parliament of the 12th November, 1415, that was now agreed to. Convocation, held at St. Paul's in November–December, 1416, granted two tenths.—Wake, *State of the Church*, 352.

[3] Sigismund of Luxemburg, king of Hungary, 1386; emperor, 1410; died 1437. He landed in England on the 1st May, and departed on the 24th August, 1416. He was made a knight of the Garter.

[4] The French fleet was investing Harfleur. The battle was fought in the Seine on the 15th August.

The Christ thou dost adore in hymns of praise,
And to angelic state thy nature raise.
Then how may I, departing hence, exceed
In lauding thee? Praise justly is thy meed." [1]

There also came into England, for the stablishing of the said peace, the duke of Holland [2], who also, the business

---

[1] The Latin verses occur in Elmham's "Liber Metricus," ll. 925–7; and also in the *Gesta Henrici Quinti*, p. 93. They are quoted by Capgrave, *De illustribus Henricis* (Rolls series), ed. Hingeston, 120; and are translated in his *Chronicle of England* (Rolls series), 314:—
"Sone aftir that the emperoure went oute of Ynglond, and in his goyng he mad his servauntis for to throwe billis in the wey, in whech was writyn swech sentens:—

'Farewel, with glorious victory,
Blessid Inglond, ful of melody.
Thou may be cleped of angel nature,
Thou servist God with so bysy cure.
We leve with the this praising,
Whech we schal evir sey and sing.' "

In an interesting letter, 2nd February, 1417, written to the king, in English, by John Forester, present at the council of Constance, the return of Sigismund to Constance is described, and his friendly feeling towards England expressed: "Lykyth now to wyte that the Wodnesday, the thyrde our efter noon, other ner therby, the sevene and twenty day of Januer, ʒour broder, Gracious Pryns, the kyng of Rome, entride the cite of Constaunce wyth ʒour lyvere of the coler abowte his necke (a glad syghte to alle ʒour lyge men to se) wyth a solempne procession of all estayts . . . and he resseyvede ʒour lordes graciously wyth reyght god cher, and of alle the worschypful men of ʒour nation he touchyde thar handys only in alle the grete prees. . . . And onde the morwe . . . he made a colation to our nation . . . and he rehersede ther how the bretherred bygan wyth hym and my Lord ʒour Fader, and how hyt is now so continuid and knyt for ʒow and ʒowr successoures, wyth the grace of God, for ever; and he tolde thame so gret worschyp of ʒowr Ryal Person, and sythyn of alle my Lordis ʒour brethers, and thenne of the governaunce of holy kyrk, dyvyn servise, operaments, and alle stat ther of kepyd, as ʒoff hit wer in paradys, in comparison to ony place that he evere came inne to for; so that, fro the heyeste unto the loweste, he commendit ʒour glorious and gracious Persone, ʒour reme, and ʒour gode governance."—*Fœdera*, ix. 434–5.

[2] William of Bavaria, count of Holland, landed in England about the 26th May and departed on the 21st June. Next year he had

A.D. 1416.  unaccomplished, soon afterwards was subtly poisoned and thus perished.

A.D. 1417.  In the year next following, that is, in the year of our Lord 1417, a parliament and convocation were holden in London; wherein the clergy and people were taxed by a levy of two tenths and as many fifteenths [1].

At last, the council having met in the month of May at Reading [2], there went out a decree from Cæsar that all the world of men with money should be set down by name; and so being summoned they emptied their coffers.

Then the lord our king turned his course with a mighty host against Normandy, to subdue it; the Irish first of all being forbidden the realm [3]. And in his passage he broke up the French fleet which threatened him; and yet the army lay on the sea-coast, awaiting a fair wind, and distressed the country-side in no small degree by levy of supplies [4].

The Scots who had gathered together in a multitude under the duke of Albany, their king, who before had been taken captive on the seas, being still a prisoner in England, were put to flight [5].

a quarrel with Sigismund, who had demanded a subsidy from the Frisians, which William forbade. His sudden death on the 31st May, 1417, was, according to the usual practice of the time, attributed to poison.

[1] Parliament met on the 16th November, 1417, and granted two tenths and two fifteenths. Convocation of Canterbury gave two tenths; that of York, one tenth.

[2] Henry was at Reading on the 10th and 11th May.—*Fœdera*, ix. 453.

[3] This seems to be a distorted account of the recall to Ireland of Irish then in England, 26th Feb., 1417.—*Proc. and Ord. Privy Council*, ij. 219.

[4] At the end of June the earl of Huntingdon was sent with a squadron to clear the Channel. He fell in with a squadron of nine Genoese carracks, and after a severe struggle captured four of them and dispersed the rest. Henry embarked at Portsmouth on the 23rd July; but a week passed before he landed in Normandy.

[5] In October, 1417, the Scots, under the duke of Albany, laid siege

The king landing in Normandy [1] at Caen, where William A.D. 1417. the conqueror lies buried, subdued the land as far as the south bank of the river Seine, taking two and thirty cities, castles, towns, and fortalices. But at the siege of Falaise [2], by the carelessness of the lord Talbot, he lost more than five hundred men who were slain by the captain of Cherbourg [3]. The booty taken in Normandy was put up to sale in every quarter of England.

Sir John Oldcastle, the heretic, renouncing the sacrament of the altar, the Blessed Virgin, and confession, and eager to pervert the king and the kingdom, after a long exile in Powis, was captured by the lord of that country, who had great reward; and in the parliament and convocation, wherein also two tenths and two fifteenths were granted in aid to the king, he was presented; and on the fourteenth day of December he was hung on the gallows in a chain of iron, after that he had been drawn, and once and for all was burnt up with fierce fire there bestowed, paying justly the penalty of both swords [4].

After the schism of thirty years' duration, which distracted Christendom, there being sometimes four, sometimes three, sometimes two popes sitting, Otto di Colonna, a noble of Rome and a Ghibelline, cardinal deacon of the title of Saint George in the Velabrum, was by all the cardinals and proctors of the several nations, with one

to Berwick; but were driven off by the earl of Northumberland. The earl of Douglas also attempted Roxburgh.

[1] At Touques, on the 1st August. Caen was besieged and carried by assault on the 4th September.

[2] Falaise was besieged from the beginning of December, 1417, and surrendered on the 2nd January, 1418.

[3] Gilbert, baron Talbot, led a raid into the Côtentin; but on his return he was attacked at the ford of St. Clement, at the mouth of the river Vire, and barely escaped with the loss of nearly all his men. See the *Chronique de Normandie*, printed at the end of the *Gesta Henrici Quinti*, p. 180.

[4] He was brought before parliament on the 14th December, and was condemned and executed in St. Giles's Fields on the same day.

A.D. 1417. accord and by miracle, the Holy Ghost moving them, chosen for pope, on Saint Martin's day (11th November); and for that reason he was called Martin the fifth.

In the same convocation last holden, spiritual patrons were constrained, under Henry Chicheley, archbishop of Canterbury, to promote graduates [1]; and he too then consecrated bishops master John Chaundeler, elect of Salisbury, and master Edmund Lacy, elect of Hereford (and I was sponsor there), after he had first confirmed them [2].

The king [3], with the manhood of the realm and with warlike valour, returned again into Normandy; and on the

A.D. 1419. nineteenth day of January, after toilsome siege and many assaults, he victoriously subdued the great city of Rouen, together with the country round about, the wretched Frenchmen not daring to stand against him, and the citizens redeeming their lives for fifty thousand pounds in gold [4]. On which account in London were made solemn processions of triumph through the city, with dancing, by clergy and people, from the shrine of Saint Erkenwald to the shrine of Saint Edward, not once only but each Wednesday and Friday.

Likewise our lord the king, with the manhood of the kingdom, in the glory of war bent his course against France, to subdue it; and within the space of two years he overcame it, with its cities and castles and strong places

A.D. 1420. whatsoever. He also made subject to his lordship the king

---

[1] An ordinance was passed, 6th November, for the due promotion of graduates, in order to encourage those who, for the advancement of learning by constant study, had continued in the universities and had grown old in academical life.—Goodwin, *Hist. Hen. V.*, 171.

[2] John Chaundeler, bishop of Salisbury, 1417–1426; and Edmund Lacy, bishop of Hereford, 1417, translated to Exeter, 1420, died 1455.

[3] The rest of Adam's text consists rather of notes than consecutive history. Here he repeats the invasion of France, and he does so again in the next paragraph.

[4] The siege of Rouen began on the 29th July, 1418, and lasted till the 19th January, 1419. The ransom imposed was 300,000 French crowns or £50,000.

and queen of France and their daughter Katharine, to be A.D. 1420.
joined to him in marriage[1], and the kingdom too, to come to
him after the death of the king, and all the magnates of the
realm. And therefore he subscribed his name in his letters
as heir and regent of France. And returning thence, with A.D. 1421.
the same lady his wife, into England for her coronation[2],
he left his brother, the duke of Clarence, to be his lieutenant
in France. But a sickness of the flux delayed this business. And a certain putative and so-called son of the king
of France, by name the Dauphin, and by the queen declared false offspring, making a party for his rights, drew
unto himself the counts of Penthievre and Armagnac and
certain Scots, and on the eve of Easter, then falling on the
twenty-third day of March, in the year of our Lord
1420-1, with great slaughter he destroyed the said duke,
in a sudden onset, along with his company in their arms
and trappings, to wit, the earls of Suffolk and Somerset
and Huntingdon, the lords of Kyme and Tankerville, and
many other noblemen, to the sore grief of England[3]. This
slaughter the earl of Salisbury, who was appointed to
ward the land along with his comrades, has cruelly avenged
with fire and sword, and is still avenging it[4]. And, seeking

[1] The treaty of Troyes was signed on the 21st May, 1420. Henry
and Katharine were immediately married in the cathedral of Troyes
on Trinity Sunday, 2nd June.

[2] They landed at Dover on the 2nd February, 1421. Katharine was
crowned on the 23rd of the month.

[3] The battle of Baugé, in Maine, took place on the 22nd March,
1421. The duke of Clarence precipitated the attack with his cavalry,
first driving in the Scottish outposts, but being then overwhelmed
by the main body before his infantry could come up. Adam blunders
in his list of the dead. The duke, John, baron de Roos, Gilbert de
Umfreville, styled earl of Kyme, and John Grey of Heton, styled earl
of Tankerville, were slain. John Beaufort, earl of Somerset, John
Holland, earl of Huntingdon, and Walter, baron Fitz-Walter, were
taken prisoners.

[4] The earl of Salisbury, governor of Normandy, failed to relieve
Alençon, to which the French had at once laid siege; but he afterwards advanced and harried the country up to Angers. See Salisbury's
letter to the king, *Fœdera*, x. 131.

A.D. 1421. to avenge it yet more, our lord the king, rending every man
throughout the realm who had money, be he rich or poor [1],
designs to return again into France in full strength [2].   But,
woe is me!, mighty men and treasure of the realm will be
most miserably fordone about this business.   And in truth
the grievous taxation of the people to this end being unbearable, accompanied with murmurs and with smothered
curses among them from hatred of the burden, I pray
that my liege lord become not in the end a partaker,
together with Julius, with Asshur, with Alexander, with
Hector, with Cyrus, with Darius, with Maccabæus, of the
sword of the wrath of the Lord!   Thereon, reader, see the
decretal xxiij., question v., " Remittuntur." [3]

[1] See *Fœdera*, x. 96, and *Proc. and Ord. Privy Council*, ij. 280, for
documents respecting enforcement of loans.

[2] Henry embarked for the last time for France on the 10th June,
1421.   Adam therefore wrote the last words of his chronicle before
that date.

[3] Decretum II., caus. xxiij., quest. v., cap. xlix. : *Aliquando puniun-
tur peccata per populos divino jussu excitatos*, beginning, " Remittuntur
peccata per Dei verbum."   Adam's closing words of discontent are
very significant.

Also published by
LLANERCH:

CELTIC CROSSES OF WALES
by J. Romilly Allen.

SYMBOLISM OF THE
CELTIC CROSS
by Derek Bryce.

THE LIFE OF ST COLUMBA
by Adamnan.

TWO CELTIC SAINTS:
the lives of
NINIAN & KENTIGERN
by Ailred and Joceline.

TALIESIN POEMS
translated by M. Pennar.

A HISTORY OF THE KINGS
OF ENGLAND
by Simeon of Durham.

THE BLACK BOOK
OF CARMARTHEN
translations by M. Pennar.

For a complete list,
write to:
Llanerch Enterprises,
Felinfach, Lampeter,
Dyfed, SA48 8PJ.